TIME
America's National Parks

The dawn's early light chases the traces of night from the forested hillsides of Great Smoky Mountains National Park.

Contents

100 Candles for Our National Parks

Celebrating the Centennial Year of the National Park Service

THE FOUNDING DIRECTOR OF THE National Park Service was Stephen Tyng Mather, whose long efforts to create a federal agency to preserve America's scenic spaces, indigenous wildlife and natural resources were crowned with success on Aug. 25, 1916. On that day, President Woodrow Wilson signed into law the historic act that created the National Park Service as a branch of the U.S. Department of the Interior.

When Mather died in 1930, his longtime colleague and successor as director of the NPS, Horace Albright, ordered the creation of small brass plaques commemorating Mather and sent one to be set up in every national park. The monuments' last sentence reads, "There will never come an end to the good that he has done."

As we celebrate the centennial year of the National Park Service, Albright's words have never seemed more apt. When Mather died, there were 20 national parks and 32 national monuments across the land. Today the park service protects 59 national parks that range from American Samoa in the South Pacific to Denali, the soaring mountain in central Alaska, to the Dry Tortugas islands off the Florida Keys—as well as hundreds of monuments, memorials, National Historical Parks and other spaces of irreplaceable value to Americans.

In 2015 the national parks welcomed the largest number of visitors in their history: 307,247,252. And with the added excitement of the agency's centennial celebrations taking place in 2016, there's little doubt that attendance will set another record this year.

When the National Park Service was born, its mission was to preserve America's most distinctive natural spaces. But beginning in 1933, the NPS began to protect the nation's heritage as well. Today the agency welcomes guests to Philadelphia's Independence Hall, Abraham Lincoln's birthplace, Thomas Edison's laboratory and many more treasured byways of our national life. In September 2015, a new visitor center opened its doors at the agency's most recent tribute to notable Americans, the Flight 93 National Memorial in Pennsylvania. To cover the full range of the park service's efforts, this book covers not only the magnificent parks under NPS protection but also the monuments, memorials and other cultural treasures the agency maintains.

The spirit that animated the lives of John Muir, Stephen Mather, Ansel Adams and many more supporters of the NPS is still to be found in the national parks. This volume is devoted to exploring some of the nation's favorites among them—as well as some of the most rewarding, most distant and least known of the parks. It's our hope that these pages will encourage you to celebrate the NPS centennial in the best possible way: by visiting a park near you. You'll find a trail or two to refresh your body, a friendly ranger to guide your way, nature's nourishment for your spirit—and the most spectacular backdrops for selfies on the planet. When you take the time to visit a national park—well, there won't be an end to the good it will do you.

—The Editors

Spring comes to Yosemite National Park, with the nation's highest waterfall, Yosemite Falls, surging in the background.

Guardian of the Nation's Spirit

"… to conserve the scenery and the natural and historic objects and the wild life therein and to provide for the enjoyment of the same in such manner …as will leave them unimpaired for the enjoyment of future generations."

—TEXT, THE ORGANIC ACT OF 1916
Legislation that established the National Park Service

Yellowstone National Park

"There can be nothing in the world more beautiful than the Yosemite, the groves of the giant sequoias and redwoods, the Canyon of the Colorado, the Canyon of the Yellowstone, the Three Tetons; and our people should see to it that they are preserved for their children and their children's children forever, with their majestic beauty all unmarred."

—THEODORE ROOSEVELT
Outdoor Pastimes of an American Hunter, *1905*

Arches
National Park

"I am here not only to evade for a while the clamor and filth and confusion of the cultural apparatus but also to confront, immediately and directly if it's possible, the bare bones of existence, the elemental and fundamental, the bedrock which sustains us."

—EDWARD ABBEY
Desert Solitaire, 1968

Carlsbad Caverns National Park

" I am gradually becoming impressed with the Carlsbad Caverns; they are so strange and deep in the earth that I can never feel about them as I do with things in the sun—rocks, trees ... surf and fog. "

—ANSEL ADAMS
Letter to Patricia English, his assistant

Olympic National Park

"It rains 12 feet a year here in the Hoh River Valley. Even when it's not raining, the moss in the trees drips water so regularly that it might as well be. When the tendril fingers of ocean fog part and beams of sun reach the valley, vapor clouds rise from the moist forest. The Hoh is an adventure in wet. And with the wet come the ferns and the quilt covering of greens that soak up sounds."

—John Balzar
Los Angeles Times, 2005

Grand Canyon National Park

"The glories and the beauties of form, color, and sound unite in the Grand Canyon—forms unrivaled even by the mountains, colors that vie with sunsets, and sounds that span the diapason from tempest to tinkling raindrop, from cataract to bubbling fountain."

—JOHN WESLEY POWELL
Canyons of the Colorado, 1875

U.S.S. *Arizona*, World War II
Valor in the Pacific
National Monument

66 Today we honor those who gave their lives at this place, half a
century ago … Think of how it was for these heroes of the Harbor,
men who were also husbands, fathers, brothers, sons. Imagine the
chaos of guns and smoke, flaming water, and ghastly carnage. Two
thousand, four hundred and three Americans gave their lives. But in
this haunting place, they live forever in our memory, reminding us
gently, selflessly, like chimes in the distant night. 99

—PRESIDENT GEORGE H.W. BUSH
Address, 50th anniversary of Japan's
attack on Pearl Harbor, Dec. 7, 1991

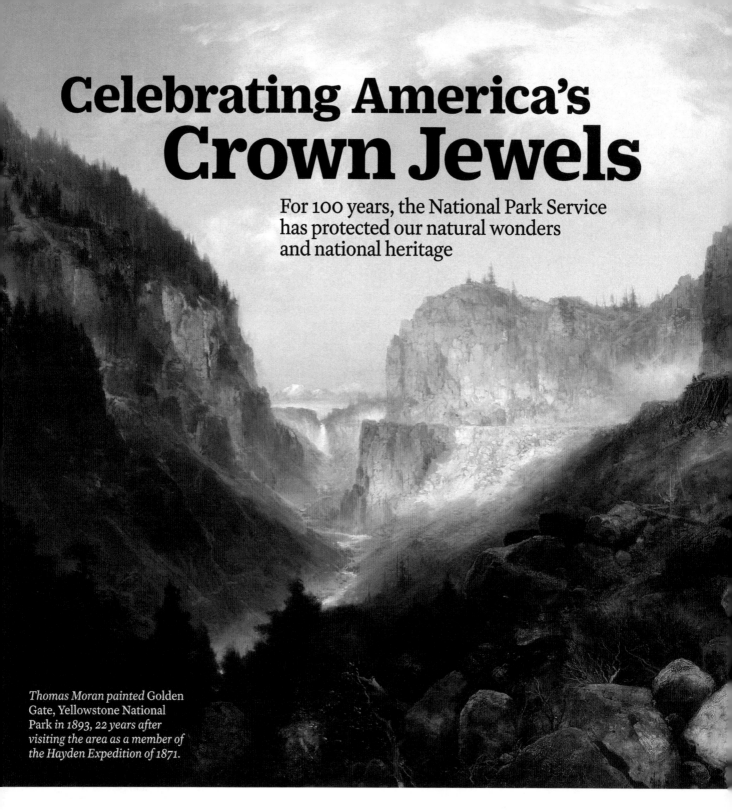

Celebrating America's
Crown Jewels

For 100 years, the National Park Service
has protected our natural wonders
and national heritage

Thomas Moran painted Golden
Gate, Yellowstone National
Park *in 1893, 22 years after
visiting the area as a member of
the Hayden Expedition of 1871.*

WHEN THE THIRD PRESIDENT of the U.S., Thomas Jefferson, struck a deal with Napoleon's France in 1803 to acquire a vast tract of land west of the Mississippi River, he set in motion a lengthy process of exploration, discovery, delight, debate and determination that would culminate in 1916 with the creation of the National Park Service (NPS)

by the 28th president, Woodrow Wilson. As the NPS celebrates its centennial in 2016, it enjoys an enviable status among government agencies: in an era when faith in many national institutions has been declining, the NPS is regarded by many Americans as the very model of a modern park system. And at a time when environmental issues have never been more critical, the NPS is a trusted, nonpartisan agency that reports to its constituents, the American public, with distinction, professionalism and

an agency to manage them was created. And even though the National Park Service now presides over an enormous realm that stretches from American Samoa in the South Pacific to Acadia National Park along the coast of Maine, the agency still seems imbued with the native spirit of the West, the land of wide-open spaces and big skies.

Two areas of scenic splendor drove the creation of the National Park Service: the Yosemite Valley in eastern California's Sierra Nevada range and the Yellowstone River region of northern Wyoming and southern Montana. Both areas were so replete with natural beauty—forests and waterfalls, towering redwoods, rushing streams and plentiful wildlife—that it seems the first instinct of those who beheld them was to vow that they must be preserved for future generations.

One such early visitor to the West's great spaces was painter George Catlin, during his 1830s journeys in the West to depict Native American life before it was submerged by the rising tide of white expansion. Catlin was perhaps the first to call for the setting aside of the West's treasures by what he called "some great protecting policy of government." He envisioned "a magnificent park . . . a nation's park, containing man and beast, in all the wild[ness] and freshness of their nature's beauty!"

The first white men to encounter the Yosemite Valley stumbled into it in 1851, three years after the discovery of gold in California launched the Gold Rush. A second group of white explorers entered the valley in 1855. Four years later, New York City newspaper editor Horace Greeley—the man who fired hearts with his famous call to action, "Go West, young man!"—was one of Yosemite's first visitors. After he marveled at the giant sequoia trees, Greeley's thoughts resembled those of painter Catlin two decades before. "If . . . the state of California does not immediately provide for the safety of these trees, I shall deeply deplore [it]," he wrote. "I am sure they will be more prized and treasured a thousand years hence than now, should they, by extreme care and caution, be preserved so long. . . ."

By the 1850s California was no longer terra incognita, thanks to the discovery of gold and the entry of the state into the Union in 1850. But the Civil War largely banished the state from the national agenda until 1864, when the eventual Union victory became ensured. That year, concerned by the effects of commercial interests on the area, prominent Californians, including Senator John Conness, managed to pass a bill, with the assistance of the Department of the Interior, establishing federal protection of the area. On June 30, 1864, President Abraham Lincoln signed Congress's Yosemite Grant Act, setting aside 39,000 acres from development, "for public use,

flair. After 100 years, the title of a 2009 Ken Burns PBS series celebrating the national parks still rings loud and true: they deserve to be called *America's Best Idea*.

The politics of creating a federal agency to preserve the majestic natural treasures of the nation may have taken place in Washington, but the impetus that drove the effort arose when Americans had their first close encounters with the spectacular wonders of the West. The first two "national parks" were born in the West, long before

This photograph of Old Faithful by Jackson uses a human figure to show the scale of Yellowstone's wonders.

resort, and recreation . . . inalienable for all time," under the custody of the State of California.

Colter's Hell The setting aside of Yosemite established a precedent for the preservation of Yellowstone, the geological wonderland in the Wyoming Territory. The first white man to explore this area was John Colter, a member of the Lewis and Clark Expedition who left the Corps of Discovery to become a fur trapper and wandered, amazed, through its unparalleled landscape of rainbow-hued mineral springs, spewing geysers and belching fumaroles in the winter of 1807–'08. When his accounts of these and other marvels circulated, they were dismissed by many as tall tales, and the area was dismissively given the nickname "Colter's Hell."

For the next decades, only fur trappers visited Yellowstone, but after the Civil War, the U.S. government began, at last, to prepare to absorb Jefferson's Louisiana Purchase into the Union. As part of that systematic ef-

fort, geologist Ferdinand V. Hayden was commissioned to lead an expedition of discovery into the Yellowstone area. When the Hayden Geological Survey of 1871 released its report, it included large-format photographs by William Henry Jackson and paintings by Thomas Moran, both expedition members, proving that John Colter's alleged tall tales were truth rather than moonshine.

Hayden was an enthusiastic advocate for Yellowstone's preservation, and he pointed to the condition of Niagara Falls in upstate New York, on the Canadian border, as an example of the misuse of a spectacular natural wonder by commercial interests: the waterfalls had become a national disgrace, a tawdry carnival of viewing platforms, souvenir stands and tourist traps. Like Catlin before him, Hayden argued for "setting aside the area [Yellowstone] as a pleasure ground for the benefit and enjoyment of the people" before commercial interests arrived to "make merchandise of these beautiful specimens."

The report created such a sensation that on March 1,

1872, President Ulysses S. Grant signed the Yellowstone Act of 1872. Thus, Yellowstone became the first U.S. government holding to be officially termed a national park—44 years before a federal agency would be created to oversee this and other American treasures.

Yosemite and Yellowstone were now poised to become the foundation of a great system of national parks, but both were poorly managed in their early years. Congress was happy to set aside Yellowstone's wonders, but funding proper upkeep was another story. The park's first supervisor, explorer and businessman Nathaniel P. Langford, was an unpaid volunteer who visited the area twice during his five-year tenure. Yellowstone received no federal funding until 1878, when a tiny budget was doled out to park management. Unable to control the area, the Department of the Interior invited the aid of the U.S. Army. In 1886 Union Civil War hero Philip Sheridan set up Camp Sheridan at Mammoth Hot Springs to help protect the park's natural riches from vandals and souvenir hunters; it became Camp Yellowstone in 1891.

Yosemite was also threatened; it had been placed in California's custody, but the state largely ignored responsibility for it. In 1875 the Michigan resort island of Mackinac was designated a "national park," but again, with little federal protection, the island became an overcrowded tourist attraction, and it was eventually returned to the state of Michigan. The tensions between the urge to preserve the nation's natural wonders and the urge to exploit them by consumer interests threatened to submerge the fledgling concept of a national park system before the idea could take root, much less blossom.

A Voice for the Parks Yellowstone and Yosemite had been saved from the profit principle, but if they were to endure and thrive, they needed a principal prophet. And right on cue, such a person arrived, in the unlikely form of a wild-haired, nature-besotted Scottish American from Wisconsin, John Muir. Attracted to botany and science from youth and deeply attuned to nature's rhythms and beauties, Muir was drawn to the West like a magnet.

A Federal Park System: Advocates and Doubters
When preservationists and conservationists clashed

John Muir

The young Muir wandered the rugged valleys of Yosemite like a monk, enraptured by nature. But after he married and became an outspoken advocate for the environment, he learned to modify his rapture.

In the 1880s and '90s Muir became one of the most compelling public voices in the nation. Americans knew he spoke for the best interests of all, not just the wealthy few.

Theodore Roosevelt

TR earned his reputation as the "conservationist president" with both words and deeds. He created the U.S. Forest Service and established 150 national forests, 51 federal bird reserves, four national game preserves, five national parks and 18 national monuments, including Arizona's unparalleled Grand Canyon, now a national park. In all, he protected some 230 million acres of public land.

Gifford Pinchot

In 1905 President Roosevelt enlisted the esteemed forester Pinchot to serve as the first chief of the new U.S. Forest Service, part of the Department of Agriculture. Pinchot called for the sustainable "conservation" of forests by logging firms, clashing with Muir, who preached untouched "preservation." At the least, their battles over the use of forests kept the green cause in the headlines.

Stephen T. Mather

Mather was the right man to serve as the first director of the National Park Service, for he circulated easily among businessmen and congressional insiders whose feelings for mountains began and ended with Capitol Hill. Mather attracted gifted associates like lawyer Horace Albright and journalist Robert S. Yard, who helped shape the reputation of both the national parks and the NPS.

His arrival in the Yosemite Valley in 1868, four years after it was set aside by Lincoln, is one of the signal moments in the history of the national parks movement.

During his first years at Yosemite, Muir was content to live like a mountain man of old, sleeping outside and roaming the woods with only a crust of bread and some loose tea in his old overcoat. But Muir wasn't just a prototype of a 1970s-era woods hippie. A gifted and disciplined scientist, he studied the park's glaciers, argued that its valleys had been carved by these rivers of ice, and became one of the world's leading experts on glaciation.

Muir was a brilliant, charismatic communicator, and after he settled down and married, he began to publish articles in the leading Eastern magazines that made him a national voice for the preservation of the wilderness. He worked throughout the 1880s to strengthen the laws that kept Yosemite free from livestock, logging and tourist attractions, culminating in the publication of two powerful articles in the influential *Century Magazine* in 1890: "The Treasure of the Yosemite" and "Features of the Proposed Yosemite National Park." Muir's arguments aroused the nation, and on Oct. 1, 1890, Congress passed a bill closely modeled on his recommendations—banning livestock grazing from Yosemite, expanding the territory it protected and naming it a national park— yet still failing to place it under federal control, as he had proposed.

Now the leading national voice for preservation and a compelling advocate for national parks, Muir realized he needed an organization to support his efforts. In 1892 he joined with fellow environmental advocates to found the Sierra Club, still a powerful advocate for green causes. Muir was named president and held that position until his death. His movement continued to win powerful allies, and in 1901, the assassination of President William McKinley thrust a prominent advocate of preservation into the presidency. Vice President Theodore Roosevelt was only 42 when he was sworn into office, and the exuberant spokesman for "the strenuous life" threw his endless energy into the fight to preserve America's grandest spaces from the predations of the businessmen he famously mocked as "malefactors of great wealth."

Roosevelt visited Muir in Yosemite on a coast-to-coast barnstorming trip in 1903, hoping to be anointed by the John the Baptist of the Sierras. A night when the two slept outdoors and woke up covered by five inches of snow seemed to do the trick: Roosevelt became the most environmentally aware of U.S. presidents, setting aside vast areas of the West from development. Acting to preserve the nation's historical treasures as well as its natural wonders, he shepherded the Antiquities Act of 1906 through Congress, giving presidents the power to create national monuments from public lands. Roosevelt quickly acted to save many of

The Tale of the Arrowhead

NPS style takes its cues from Mother Nature: organic, rough-hewn and built to last

There's nothing fancy or subtle about the familiar arrowhead logo of the National Park Service, and that's by design. The arrowhead itself is a gracious nod to the original inhabitants of North America; its elements represent the natural treasures under NPS protection. The bison at bottom is a reference to the buffalo on the Department of the Interior's logo.

Although the NPS employed midcentury design in the architecture of some of its visitor centers in the '50s, it has wisely avoided fads and fashions that eventually become dated—after all, "eventually" is a term well understood by those who are used to measuring time from the perspective of sequoias, glaciers and mountains.

The NPS takes its design cues from the parks it maintains. Rustic hues are employed, and visitor centers are often built from native woods, rocks and other local materials. Whereas NPS buildings often sport the latest in interactive designs and other technology, particularly in the agency's effort to educate younger visitors, their most important elements are generally the large windows that direct guests to the star of the show: the scenery.

The NPS website at *nps.gov* reflects the same emphasis on function over form. Its thousands of pages of helpful information are no more flashy than the arrowhead above or the old-school posters at right, but they are extensive, well-written and informative—the NPS at its best.

A Brush with Fine Art for the National Parks
The New Deal created an enduring American style for the NPS

Franklin D. Roosevelt's New Deal programs left their mark on the National Park Service in many ways, including these glorious travel posters, created under the aegis of the Works Progress Administration (WPA), an agency that employed artists, musicians and writers during the Great Depression.

The NPS posters had almost been forgotten when park ranger Doug Leen first became aware of them after finding an old poster at Grand Teton National Park in 1973. In the 1990s, Leen and Tom DuRant, an NPS archivist, helped track down copies of the original WPA posters. More recent artists have created a host of works inspired by these 1930s classics.

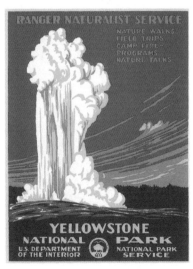

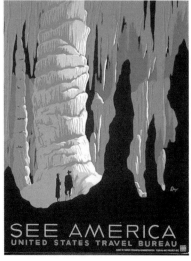

Members of the Civilian Conservation Corps set up camp in the Shenandoah Valley near Luray, Va., in 1933.

the West's crown jewels. The first national monument was Devils Tower in Wyoming; 18 others followed, including the Grand Canyon, which Roosevelt declared held major scientific interest.

The Vision Takes Shape Muir won another disciple in the wealthy San Francisco–born Stephen T. Mather, who retired from running a financial empire based on the mining of borax in Death Valley and devoted himself to the creation of a federal parks agency. By 1915 Mather was working on an unpaid basis with the Department of the Interior to demonstrate the urgent need for a law authorizing the creation of a much-enhanced system of national parks under federal control. His efforts were rewarded on Aug. 25, 1916, when Democratic president Woodrow Wilson signed the legislation that established the National Park Service.

Mather was named the first director of the NPS and was assigned a bright lawyer, Horace Albright, as an aide. The two men, with the valuable assistance of a savvy journalist, Robert S. Yard, set out to create a professional corps that would be regarded as above politics, one that would speak and act in the people's interest. Befitting an organization that would be in charge of patrolling the parks and enforcing federal laws, and recalling Fort Yel-

lowstone, the NPS retained some quasi-military aspects, including the campaign hat worn by its rangers, which remains an indelible and beloved symbol of the agency.

Mather suffered from bipolar disorder, which his love of the outdoors helped alleviate. Even so, he was a happy warrior, a jovial representative of the NPS who could talk the language of senators and representatives, if with the accent of Muir. Mather shrewdly understood that the key to wide acceptance of the new system of parks and its governing agency was to get people into the parks and to demonstrate how their magnificent scenery generated tourism. He founded new parks across the nation, and when he stepped down in 1929, the NPS oversaw 20 national parks and 32 national monuments.

Albright succeeded his old friend, and under President Franklin D. Roosevelt, the NPS was given a much broader mandate. On June 10, 1933, Roosevelt signed Executive Order 6166, which consolidated all national parks, monuments, military parks, cemeteries and memorials under the direction of the National Park Service.

In a penstroke, FDR expanded the reach and power of the NPS across the nation, adding 12 natural areas in nine Western states and Alaska, then still a territory, and 57 historical areas located in 17 predominantly Eastern states and the District of Columbia. It was a mighty big gulp to swallow, but FDR knew that: in his first weeks in office, he also won approval of a new public relief program, the Civilian Conservation Corps, which put men to work for Uncle Sam. At its peak, in 1935, the CCC operated 118 camps in the national parks, employing tens of thousands of workers to build the roads, bridges and buildings the newly enlarged system needed.

During the 1930s and '40s, the NPS devoted itself to getting its hands around its vast new holdings amid economic depression and World War II. When the war years ended, the nation expanded as never before. The economy boomed, the population grew, the movement to the suburbs began—and America's moms and dads, enjoying some extra money in their pockets for the first time in decades, could afford to buy a new station wagon and hit the road. Their destination: the national parks.

But if the parents were ready for the parks, the parks weren't ready for the parents. Recognizing the need for a system-wide upgrade of NPS facilities, director Conrad Wirth launched in 1956 a decade-long program, Mission 66, which succeeded in improving every aspect of the parks, from the roads that brought the people, to the new visitor centers that greeted and oriented them, to the infrastructure of the trails and campgrounds they used.

Mission 66 culminated on the 50th anniversary of the NPS, and the second 50 years of the service, energized by the environmental movement of the 1960s and '70s, have seen not only the expansion of its original mission, thanks to the addition of some 57 million acres to its holdings, but also a new commitment to its efforts to educate Americans on the state of the environment.

In 2015 the parks attracted more travelers than ever before: 307 million visitors. And with the NPS rolling out the green carpet in 2016 for a grand centennial celebration, the year's attendance will doubtless be even higher. Small wonder that, after 100 years, the U.S. national parks are still America's best idea and a model for countries around the world. But come to think of it, there are mighty few small wonders in the NPS system: those wonders are as high as Alaska's Denali, as deep as Arizona's Grand Canyon, and as enduring and flourishing as the sequoia trees in California's Yosemite.

Ranger Tim McNeil prepares visitors for a descent to the Balcony House ruins in Mesa Verde N.P. in Colorado.

The NPS by the Numbers

Entities protected by the NPS (a partial list)

81 National Monuments

78 National Historic Sites

59 National Parks

50 National Historical Parks

30 National Memorials

25 National Battlefields and National Battlefield Parks, Sites and Military Parks

24 National Seashores, Lakeshores, and Wild and Scenic Rivers

19 National Preserves

18 National Recreation Areas

307 million
Number of visitors to the national parks in 2015

10 Most Visited National Parks, 2015

1. Great Smoky Mountains

2. Grand Canyon

3. Rocky Mountain

4. Yosemite

5. Yellowstone

SOURCES: NPS; Time.com

Oldest

National Park
Yellowstone, Wyo., Mont., 1872

National Monument
Devils Tower, Wyo., 1906 ▼

Newest

National Park
Pinnacles, Calif., 2013

National Memorial
Flight 93 National Memorial,
Pa., 2011

National Monuments
Mojave Trails, Castle Mountains,
Sand to Snow, Calif.

8 million+
acres

Largest Park ▲

Wrangell–St. Elias, Alaska
13 million+ acres when Wrangell–St. Elias
National Preserve is included

Smallest Park

Hot Springs, Ark.
5,000 acres

6. Zion

7. Olympic

8. Grand Teton

9. Acadia

10. Glacier

Just for fun, TIME asked readers on Time.com to name their favorite national park.
The responses to our unscientific poll reflected a battle of the East and West coasts. **Olympic** in Washington
State won 28% of the 2,637 votes cast, with Maine's **Acadia** at second with 25%. The others, in order:
Grand Canyon, Yosemite, Yellowstone, Glacier, Great Smoky Mountains, Arches, Rocky Mountain, Everglades.

Preserving America's Singular Spaces

66 Keep close to Nature's heart . . . and break clear away, once in a while, and climb a mountain or spend a week in the woods. Wash your spirit clean. 99

—John Muir, quoted by Samuel Hall Young in
Alaska Days with John Muir, 1915

Rocky Mountain N.P., Colorado *A cautious climber nears the edge of Chasm View Pinnacle, high above Chasm Lake.*

The Lure of a Challenge

For millions of visitors, the parks offer inviting arenas for exercise—with a view

THEODORE ROOSEVELT, THE DYNAMIC, visionary president whose spirit still seems to inhabit our system of national parks, was an advocate of what he called "the strenuous life." He told a gathering of Chicago business executives in 1899, "I wish to preach, not the doctrine of ignoble ease, but the doctrine of the strenuous life, the life of toil and effort, of labor and strife." For Roosevelt, this meant testing one's self not only in the political arena but also in the natural arena. From boyhood, he had been an avid collector of flora and fauna, and he became a noted sportsman who loved hunting and fishing. A proud Westerner, even if an adopted one, he loved his mornings on horseback in his youthful days in the Dakota Territory.

In Roosevelt's mind, the national park system he championed would preserve the nation's wilderness regions, offering Americans the chance to exert themselves in the wild for centuries to come. And they do: the national parks offer millions of Americans a chance to explore the wide-open spaces and rough it for a spell—hiking and climbing, cycling and kayaking, spelunking and fishing. For millions of would-be Roosevelts, the parks, trails, seashores and mountaintops overseen by the National Park Service are Roosevelt's living memorial.

Because It's There Those in search of a challenge in the outdoors will find more than their share at Rocky Mountain N.P. in northern Colorado. A sort of national park system in itself, this sprawling, 265,600-acre park offers every kind of activity, from hiking, horseback riding and camping to extreme rock-climbing, as well as a beckoning array of water sports, including canoeing, kayaking, swimming and fishing. For those who aren't in good physical condition, simply traversing the terrain

here can be a strain: the park is located at an elevation more than 7,000 feet above sea level, and it may take some time for tenderfeet to acclimate themselves to the thin air in the park. But for those who do thrive in rarefied air, there are plenty of challenges to go around: the park boasts more than 60 peaks, carved by ancient glaciers, whose elevation is more than 12,000 feet.

If the sheer height of Rocky Mountain N.P. doesn't take your breath away, there's a good chance the scenery will. The park is a wonderland for wildlife photographers, with elk, mule deer, bighorn sheep and a passel of smaller critters—marmots, chipmunks, porcupines and snowshoe hares—ready for their close-up.

Small wonder the park attracted 4.1 million visitors in

A visitor sets his sights on a bull elk that seems happy to strike a pose at Rocky Mountain National Park.

Gates of the Arctic N.P., Alaska *A lead dog gives voice to the call of the wild as a dogsledder enjoys the ride.*

2015, an increase of 21% over 2014. Rangers credited the surge in attendance to the low cost of gas, an increase in the local population—and the chance for visitors with a special devotion to Rocky Mountain N.P. to celebrate its centennial; the park was formally dedicated in September 1915, a year before the National Park Service as we know it today was authorized.

North to Alaska For many lovers of the outdoor life, the road to adventure heads northwest. Separated by geography from the Lower 48 states of the U.S., Alaska is a kingdom unto itself, a vast domain that is both the largest state in the union and its least densely populated. Some 735,000 people call themselves Alaskans, and roughly 40% of them live in the city of Anchorage, in the state's southernmost region, where many of the state's settled areas are clustered.

Alaska's interior is thus an immense range of nature, much of it untouched by the hand of man. The NPS operates eight national parks in Alaska: Denali, Wrangell–St. Elias, Glacier Bay, Lake Clark, Kenai Fjords, Katmai, Kobuk Valley and Gates of the Arctic. A number of the parks also function as national wildlife preserves. In all, these NPS holdings take up 54 million acres of the state's land and compose some 60% of the total U.S. land occupied by NPS parks. All that space creates room for lots of adventure, and Alaska's parks draw hunters and fishermen, kayakers, hikers and mountain climbers. Naturalists, bird-watchers and wild-animal photographers also treasure the vast, unspoiled spaces of these northern parks—

> THE UNION'S LARGEST STATE IS ALSO ITS LEAST DENSELY POPULATED

as do the hardy souls who mush their huskies through winter's snowy realm, practicing for Alaska's signature sporting event, the annual Iditarod Trail Sled Dog Race from Anchorage to Nome. Even though most visitors arrive during the brief summer months, there's room for all comers in this northern kingdom that U.S. secretary of state William Seward negotiated to purchase from imperial Russia in 1867—for $7.2 million—in one of history's greatest real estate bargains.

Burros, Descending Although it's an iconic American endurance test, muscling a pack of sled dogs across Alaska's vast, snowy expanses is an adventure most of us will never get to enjoy. But it's a rare citizen who hasn't dreamed of making one of the archetypal national parks journeys, the downhill descent from the top of the Grand

Canyon to the Colorado River at its bottom—while rocking back and forth on the back of a mule.

A burro ride into the Grand Canyon is not only a lesson in geology, it's also a trip back into the nation's past. More than 600,000 riders have saddled up and explored the wonders of the Grand Canyon since the guided tours were first offered in the late 1870s. The much-put-upon mules are famously sure-footed, but there are limits to their tolerance: a top weight of 200 pounds is imposed on riders who descend to the canyon's bottom. The rides are very popular: wannabe buckaroos should reserve a burro well in advance.

The classic man-meets-mule experience involves a ride to the base of the Grand Canyon and an overnight stay at legendary Phantom Ranch. But it takes two days and one night to complete—and anyone with a fear of heights should avoid it. Those who prefer a calmer encounter with a mule can enjoy a new four-mile, three-hour ride along the eastern rim of the canyon that offers striking views sans the dizzying descent.

Visitors who prefer a little more speed in their giddy-up can experience a thrilling river-rafting adventure on the Colorado, giving modern Americans a chance to share the wonder of geologist and explorer John Wesley Powell and his comrades felt as they charted the canyons of the Colorado River in their 1869 mission of exploration. "We are three quarters of a mile in the depths of the earth," Powell wrote, "and the great river shrinks into insignificance as it dashes its angry waves against the walls

Grand Canyon N.P., Arizona *Riders ascend the trail to the rim of the Grand Canyon during their close encounter with a long-eared equine.*

and cliffs, that rise to the world above; they are but puny ripples, and we are but pygmies, running up and down the sands, or lost among the boulders."

The Art of the Arches Not far upstream from the Grand Canyon, outside Moab, Utah, the Colorado River passes along the southern edge of one of the nation's most unusual natural spaces, Arches N.P. Here, over tens of thousands of years, geological forces laid down a

Arches N.P., Utah
Campers settle in for the night beneath a sandstone span.

Carlsbad Caverns N.P., New Mexico *Its depths are measureless to man, for new chambers are still being discovered.*

deep bed of salt, then covered it with layers of sandstone, ranging from buff tans to a surprisingly vivid salmon color. The weight of the sandstone often forced the salt beneath it to rise and form domes of salt. Then, over long ages, winds eroded the softer sandstone and left the more durable rock, which was then hewed by the high-desert winds into the most fantastic of natural geometries: high, rounded arches and lower, longer arches—more than 2,000 arches in all.

These "windows," as the area's early settlers called them, are interspersed with other geological spectacles: tall columns, spires and pinnacles, as well as giant boulders delicately balanced, one atop the other.

Arches N.P. attracts visitors who travel the old-fashioned way, one step at a time. No canoes, rafts or kayaks traverse this dry desert landscape, and there are no packs of mules or riders to be seen. Indeed, though humans have wandered through these lands for some 10,000 years, any marks they may have left have been scoured away by the winds that shaped the arches, leaving spectacular visions of nature's powers, frozen in time.

Arches weighs in at No. 16 of the nation's 20 most-visited national parks, with more than 1.4 million visitors in 2015. A lucky few of them will make reservations in advance and snag one of the 50 campsites located in the Devils Garden Campground about 18 miles from the park entrance.

A Roofed Canyon Some of the most marvelous sights in the American West lie not aboveground but beneath it, and they attract a special breed of visitors, those attuned to the allure of caves. The celebrated humorist Will Rogers memorably summed up the magnetic appeal of Carlsbad Caverns National Park in New Mexico after a tour of the vast underground domain: it is, he said, "the Grand Canyon with a roof on it."

The primary attractions at Carlsbad are its magnificent formations of stalactites and stalagmites, but a close second are the hundreds of thousands of bats that call the caverns home. Like Kentucky's Mammoth Cave N.P., the sprawling cavern's depths are still being probed. As recently as Oct. 31, 2013, a cave technician and park volunteer discovered a new chamber above Carlsbad's famed Big Room, its largest chamber; the unexpected space, about 100 feet in diameter, was quickly dubbed Halloween Hall.

> **CARLSBAD CAVERNS' NEW CHAMBER: HALLOWEEN HALL**

A River Runs Through It Ask a friend to name the most visited of America's 58 national parks, and you're liable to hear the same guesses: Yosemite, Yellowstone, Grand Canyon, Arches, Glacier and the other iconic parks of the nation's West. In fact, the answer is a park that lies east of the Mississippi, straddling the southern Appalachian Mountains in North Carolina and Tennessee: Great Smoky Mountains National Park.

Each year, more than 10 million visitors descend upon—or, more accurately, ascend to—this heavily forested park in the Appalachian Mountains to enjoy magnificent vistas, exhilarating hikes and, not least, a good day's fishing. The park is home to 700 to 800 miles of rushing streams to cast a fly into; it's one of the most popular fly-fishing regions east of the Mississippi. For many fly-casters, the prize catch here is trout, but smallmouth bass are another popular

> GREAT SMOKY
> MOUNTAINS
> PARK IS PRIZED
> BY FLY-FISHING
> ANGLERS

target for the avid anglers of the sprawling park.

Other prime national parks for fishing include Yellowstone, Olympic and Glacier. Those in search of a more unusual—and definitely challenging—fishing adventure can try Voyageurs N.P. in northern Minnesota, on the Canadian border, where the fish (and mosquitoes) are always biting during the short summers, while the winter months bring long spells of frigid weather that offer an opportunity for serious ice-fishing in the Land of 10,000 Lakes.

Two parks on the East Coast offer anglers a chance to sample both freshwater and saltwater fishing. Maine's gorgeous Acadia N.P., on the Atlantic Coast, offers fishing for salmon and trout in mountain lakes and ponds, including those on Mount Desert Island, as well as saltwater fishing for mackerel, striped bass and bluefish. A long way down the coast, Florida's Everglades N.P.

Great Smoky Mountains N.P., North Carolina *A fisherman casts his fly in the park that straddles two states.*

North Cascades N.P., Washington State *Above, hikers tramp along the Pacific Crest Trail. At the other side of the continent, left, a group celebrates its arrival at the northern terminus of the Appalachian Trail.*

2012 memoir *Wild*, which tells the story of her 1,100-mile tramp along the Pacific Crest Trail in 1995, when she was 26 years old. That's a lot of footsteps, yet it's less than one half the trail's length: it runs 2,650 miles from the Canadian border to the Mexican border.

When Strayed's popular book was turned into a Hollywood film starring Reese Witherspoon, the spotlight on the Pacific Crest Trail ignited interest in a beautiful national trail known to and loved by many on the West Coast but not nearly as well known to most Americans as its Eastern counterpart, the Appalachian Trail. (That trail got its own boost of publicity in 2015, when a film version of Bill Bryson's 1998 book *A Walk in the Woods* attracted flocks of hikers to its paths.)

The Pacific Crest Trail offers an example of various entities working together to serve the public. It is administered by the U.S. Forest Service but includes sections under the management of the NPS, the Bureau of Land Management, the California State Parks and the Pacific Crest Trail Association. The trail has become so popular since the film's premiere, in December 2014, that authorities have been forced to regulate access to

gives anglers a chance to fish in one of the world's most unique environments, where largemouth bass are plentiful in the freshwater streams, while the park's saltwater mangrove swamps are the lair of the elusive snook.

Tales of the Trail Strolling a few miles along a river rich in fishing holes or along a well-marked NPS trail is a satisfying journey for most of us. But for others, hiking is a calling, one best satisfied over the course of a months-long trek that can cover thousands of miles. Such long-distance hikes have enjoyed a renaissance in recent years, thanks to the success of writer Cheryl Strayed's

it. Veteran hikers call it "the *Wild* effect," and some of them, predictably, grumble at the tenderfeet they fear will ruin the solitary pleasures of a ramble on the trail.

But members of the Pacific Crest Trail Association, a nonprofit organized to "protect, preserve and promote" the trail, have welcomed the publicity from Strayed's book. The group published a special "*Wild* edition" of its magazine, has highlighted hikes featured in the book and film, and has partnered with Strayed on a campaign called *#ResponsiblyWILD,* which is intended to teach hikers to be safe and aware of others' needs on the trail.

Tech Steps In Yes, the park system is intended to preserve nature in its original state, but there is no stopping the advance of progress, and over the years the ways we interact with our national parks have been transformed. New, lightweight materials have given climbers and campers far lighter gear to carry on their travels. Cellphones keep hikers in touch, even when they're out of visual range, can relay critical weather advisories when needed, and boast lifesaving GPS navigation apps.

The advent of the smartphone put not only a camera but an entire editing suite in people's pockets, making it simpler than ever for amateurs to take a picture, crop and enhance it in myriad ways, and save it in digital form. One result: more and more Americans are visiting the parks to capture images of animals in the wild. NPS officials understand their visitors and have placed only a few common-sense restrictions on picture-taking.

Technology has changed the ways we interact with nature in many other ways. Consider the humble kayak, the slim, small canoe pioneered by the Inuit and other

> TECHNOLOGY IS CHANGING THE WAY WE EXPERIENCE OUR PARKS

indigenous polar peoples. In recent years the popularity of these simple nautical get-arounds has exploded. Today's kayaks are far stronger, lighter and more maneuverable than their predecessors, and they have created an entirely new way for people to travel the nation's rivers, lakes and seashores. (The latest craze: kayak fishing.)

The popularity of kayaking has been driven, in part, by the accessibility of inviting and challenging waters in which to paddle. For most Americans, a national park that offers the test of whitewater kayaking is no more than a couple of hours' drive from home. Even residents of the nation's capital can find a serious whitewater challenge only 11 miles upstream from Washington, at the Great Falls of the Potomac River.

Administered by the NPS but not authorized as a national park, the Great Falls are a tough test for the most

practiced of kayakers. Here the Potomac narrows dramatically, from a width of 1,000 feet to only 60 to 100 feet, speeding up the river's pace just as kayakers approach the boulder-strewn Mather Gorge, named in honor of Stephen T. Mather, the first director of the NPS. As kayakers descend through a vertical drop of 76 feet in only a mile, paddles flash as boaters fight the whitewater rapids to keep themselves upright. Like so many Americans, they have fallen hard for the strenuous challenges offered by the nation's great parks.

Great Falls Park *A kayaker braves the steepest drop at the river, which runs between Virginia and Maryland.*

Profile: Tommy Caldwell and Kevin Jorgeson

Cliffhangers on El Capitan

Two gutsy climbers ascend Yosemite's toughest cliff—without tools

TO UNDERSTAND THE EXTENT OF THE feat achieved by rock climbers Tommy Caldwell, 36, and Kevin Jorgeson, 30, on Jan. 14, 2015, you may need a bit of background. The setting for their adventure was the Dawn Wall of El Capitan in the Yosemite Valley, one of the world's most challenging climbing sites. A solid-granite prominence that thrusts like an extended finger 3,000 feet into the air from the floor of the valley, the Dawn Wall is a study in verticality that got its name because it is the first rock outcrop in the valley to catch the rays of the morning sun. It's no Mount Everest, but its sheer rock cliffs make it one of the most daunting climbing challenges in the world, and over the decades the greatest mountaineers on the planet have tackled it, creating a tangle of different paths to the summit.

The next thing it helps to know is the unusual equipment used by Caldwell and Jorgeson on their history-making climb: their bare hands and sneaker-clad feet. Period. The two are "free climbers," daring souls who

tackle the steep cliffs without using any of the support tools of most climbers: pitons and hammers, ropes and nylon ladders. Yes, they wear belaying ropes so their partner can stop their descent in midair should they fall—or, more accurately, *when* they fall, for that's part of the process. (Ascending without ropes of any kind is a highly risky endeavor, known as "free-soloing.") Per the rules of free-climbing, each pitch cannot be considered achieved until it is completed in a single climb, without falling. When you fall, you start the pitch all over again.

Since part of the challenge was to remain on the Dawn Wall's face until they reached the summit, the two slept on portaledges, 6-foot-by-4-foot sleeping platforms hammered into position on the sheer rock face. Room service was provided by friends who would ascend to their series of suspended base camps—or base ledges—every couple of days to provide sustenance: bagels, salmon, salami, coffee, whiskey and life's other necessities.

Here's the last thing you need to know: rock climbers

divide cliffs into a series of rope lengths, or pitches, and each pitch is slightly less than 100 feet in length. The Dawn Wall consisted of 32 pitches, each of which had to be mastered before the next could be tackled.

In preparation for their ascent, Caldwell spent a year examining the face of the Dawn Wall, tracing every minute detail of its surface in search of cracks and outcrops that might offer hand- and footholds for the climb to come, and drilling holes for the belaying ropes. On Dec. 27, 2014, the two men set out on their uphill journey. They scrabbled up the lower pitches in record time, even though they are among the toughest climbs on the face, drawing on their familiarity with them—for this was the duo's sixth attempt at free-climbing the Dawn Wall.

Moving quickly, Caldwell and Jorgeson got to Pitch 14 in the first six days, two pitches farther than they had ever reached before. Caldwell, the more experienced of the two, just kept climbing, reaching Pitch 20 after two weeks on the wall. But Jorgeson bogged down at an old nemesis, Pitch 15, falling repeatedly when his hands or feet lost their grip on the cliff face.

For 10 days, Jorgeson struggled to surmount Pitch 15, falling on every attempt, even as his hands grew bloodier and each grip became more painful. But finally, on January 9, he reached the top of the pitch. Later, he said of this climb, "The conditions were just magic. It was the one moment over the last 10 days when it was actually cloudy and cold enough to climb during daylight. It all lined up to create this one moment in which my skin was good enough and the conditions were perfect." Yes, for much of their ascent, the two climbed mainly at night, for the days were too hot and their bodies too sweaty to climb—work so fine-grained that at times they brushed loose grit from handholds with toothbrushes.

Energized by his conquest of Pitch 15, Jorgeson made quick work of Pitch 16, where he had fallen and sustained a serious injury in a previous climb. He soon caught up with Caldwell, and the two men completed their ascent of the Dawn Wall's last pitches around 3:25 p.m. on Jan. 14, 2015. They were greeted by cheering supporters and a cadre of reporters and photographers, for their quest to free-climb El Capitan's toughest face had generated worldwide buzz, thanks to breathtaking photos of their progress as well as the tweets and posts on social media they had sent during their adventure. Responding to one tweet, Jorgeson rejected congratulations that the two men hoped to "conquer" the Dawn Wall. "This is not about an effort to 'conquer,'" he said, perhaps humbled by nature's power. "It's about realizing a dream."

Sheer guts: Caldwell, suspended, and Jorgeson, on a portaledge, lived on the face for 19 days, chasing their dream.

Preserving Exotic
Ecosystems

The parks are laboratories where scientists
and rangers collaborate to protect the planet

OUR NATIONAL PARKS SERVE AS SANC-
tuaries for the soul, playgrounds for
families, arenas for adventurers and
eye candy for camera-toting tourists.
But one of their most important functions is less immediately apparent:
as home to some of the most exotic ecosystems on the
planet, the parks serve as living laboratories where scientists, rangers and volunteers explore the delicate web
that connects humans and animals, nature and society,
the climate and the planet.

The founders of the parks always believed that the
lands they were preserving from development would en-
rich our souls. But the idea that these reserves could also
expand our knowledge was late in arriving, tracking the
development of today's ecological consciousness. After
all, the term "ecosystem" was not coined until the 1930s
and did not come into wide use until the 1950s. Today,
amid global climate change, the state of our environment
has become one of the dominant issues of the age, and
the parks are in the vanguard of ecological studies.

The Goats of Glacier For tourists, Glacier N.P. is syn-
onymous with scenic splendor. But scientists regard it
in a completely different way: to them, it is the capstone
of the Crown of the Continent Ecosystem, a biologically
rich environment that stretches across 28,000 square
miles of land in two nations, ranging from the Upper Elk
and Upper Highwood rivers in western Canada to Montana's Blackfoot Valley in the U.S., some 250 miles south.

Glacier N.P., Montana *Catch me if you can: when
predators come calling, sure-footed mountain goats can
take refuge in the vertical world of their cliffside salt licks.*

This magnificent alpine ecosystem, home to lofty
peaks, river-carved valleys and broad prairie lands, supports 1,000 native plants, 70 mammals and 260 species
of birds. Here wildlife specialists are studying the effects
of human interaction on the animals that roam Glacier,
which is primarily in Montana and nudges into Wyoming.

As Glacier ranger Denise Germann playfully admit-
ted to TIME, "There's some concern that we know less
about goats than we think we do." So, in a three-year
project that began in the summer of 2013, Glacier personnel, in partnership with wildlife scientists at the University of Montana and the Montana state parks, began
studying the habits of the beautiful and exceptionally
sure-footed snow-white mountain goats that make their
home amid the sheer walls of Glacier's cliffs and ravines.
Their goal: to track the goats' movements through the
park and to measure the differences in behavior between those goats that have become habituated to human presence and those that have experienced little
contact with humans.

All told, there are believed to be some 1,500 goats in
the park. In 2013 researchers put six goats to sleep with
dart guns and placed radio collars on them to track their
locations. GPS radio collars, which can cost up to $3,000
apiece and are donated by organizations that support
park activities, record each goat's location every few
hours and send the data, via satellite, to a scientist's com-
puter. After three years, an internal clock in the collar
orders it to disengage, and it drops to the ground to be
collected by a ranger or researcher.

Data from the first year of the study allowed rangers
and scientists to pinpoint, for the first time, the goats'
wintertime range within the park and showed that some
goats have indeed become habituated to human intru-

sion. Result: they altered their herding behavior and changed their grazing habits, venturing into meadows and forests to forage, whereas less habituated goats generally preferred to remain near the rocky, narrow cliffs and ledges where they are at home—and humans and predators are not.

As Germann explained, mountain goats have been the iconic animal of Glacier since the park was founded in 1910; the Great Northern Railway Co., which strongly supported the creation of the park as a magnet for tourists, featured a mountain goat as its logo. Studying the relationship between goats and humans is the best way to ensure that these nimble creatures will still be showing off their climbing skills in 2116.

The Yellowstone Caldera No national park is more famed for its exotic ecosystem than is Yellowstone. Though the park, which spreads across Wyoming into parts of Idaho and Montana, is home to splendid wildlife and magnificent scenery, its bizarre geology is its most entrancing aspect: roaring geysers erupt with eerie predictability; steaming mineral pools are more vibrant than a rainbow; smoking fumaroles open on canyon floors, resembling doors into the underworld.

Geologists have long known that Yellowstone's eerie landscape is the product of tectonic forces working beneath the surface of the earth. But only in recent decades have they come to understand precisely how vast those forces can be. Yellowstone, geologists explain, is a "hot spot," where the giant plates of the planet's crust pass over a colossal reservoir of volcanic magma that is unusually close to the Earth's surface. Yellowstone, it turns out, lies within the radius of a giant, 30-by-45-mile caldera of a subterranean supervolcano. Someday it will erupt, as it has done an estimated 140 times in the past, including some 2 million, 1.2 million and, most recently, 640,000 years ago. Every year, seismologists track 1,000 to 3,000 earthquakes beneath Yellowstone, evidence of the intense geological activity that fuels the park's wonders.

> YELLOWSTONE N.P. STRADDLES AN IMMENSE UNDERGROUND SUPERVOLCANO

Yellowstone N.P., Wyoming *The colors in Yellowstone's Grand Prismatic Spring are created when tiny organisms, bacteria and archaea interact with its hot, mineral-rich water.*

Joshua Tree N.P., California *Legend holds that Mormon pioneers gave the Joshua tree its name, likening its outstretched arms, above, to those of the biblical prophet.*

At near right, a saguaro cactus blooms; at far right, a desert spiny lizard sunbathes. Reptiles are well adapted to arid, hot ecosystems.

The scare factor of a big blow-up at Yellowstone seemed to increase a bit when researchers at the University of Utah reported in an April 2015 paper that they had discovered a gigantic, previously unknown chamber of magma beneath the park. This reservoir of hot and, in some places, liquid rock is big enough to fill the Grand Canyon 11 times over. Such an eruption would be cataclysmic beyond imagining, but veteran University of Utah geologist Robert B. Smith, a co-author of the paper, reminded readers that the daily odds of such an occurrence are about 700,000 to 1 and pointed out that the discovery of the chamber has not altered that fact. "The actual hazard is the same," he declared, "but now we have a much better understanding of the complete crustal magma system." Feel better now?

IN SOME YEARS, 3,000 MINOR EARTHQUAKES OCCUR AT YELLOWSTONE

Like Yellowstone, Joshua Tree N.P., some 140 miles east of Los Angeles, is also a hot spot these days. But the heat isn't coming from beneath the earth: it is a product of rising temperatures and lack of rain. Joshua Tree is a desert ecosystem, where cactus and succulents are the prevailing flora, and the local critters are well adapted to the park's climate. The largest of them—bighorn sheep, coyotes, black-tailed jackrabbits and kangaroo rats—are nocturnal. Reptiles, including snakes and lizards, are more active during the daytime, but they spend a good deal of their time in burrows, avoiding direct exposure to the sun, and some of them hibernate in the winter.

But even this desert ecosystem is imperiled by the combination of slowly rising temperatures and drought conditions that have struck the park in recent years. And it's the park's titular specimen, the Joshua tree, that is suffering the most. Scientists know the Joshua as *Yucca brevifolia*, and they're quick to remind you that its common name is a misnomer: a Joshua tree isn't really a tree; it's a succulent. Like another elder of the Southwestern desert, the sturdy saguaro cactus, Joshua trees can grow to a compelling height; some of them raise their arms 40 feet into the dry desert air. And they're as long-lived as the saguaro, standing tall for more than 200 years.

> **A TYPICAL JOSHUA TREE CAN LIVE FOR MORE THAN 200 YEARS**

A Joshua tree's long life makes it hard to measure the effects of climate change upon it over a short span of time. But in 2015, scientists at the park and the U.S. Fish and Wildlife Service and a research team led by University of California, Riverside, ecologist Cameron Barrows organized the first long-term project designed to monitor the trees' responses to climate change and drought. Barrows's team hopes to establish a baseline portrait of the state of the trees today, amid fears that rising temperatures and diminished rain may force them into higher, cooler ground, losing as much as 90% of their current range. And since each tree is the center of its own miniature ecosystem, one that supports

Katmai N.P., Alaska
Bears scan the river for migrating salmon at Brooks Falls in southwest Alaska.

butterflies, moths, great horned owls and some 20 other species of birds, a decline in the Joshua tree population may spell doom for millions of creatures. For now, park officials estimate that there are some 2.5 million trees in the park's 800,000 acres.

Lights, Bearcam, Action! Far from prismatic mineral springs, Joshua trees and spiny lizards, the national parks of Alaska embrace a variety of ecosystems, from alpine heights to the state's sweeping lowlands, classified as taiga and tundra. This vast realm of grasslands, coniferous forests and lichen-topped rocks is visually splendid and home to millions of animals, including caribou, moose, bears,

> **22 MILLION VIEWERS SAW BEARS FISH FOR SALMON IN 2015**

foxes, arctic wolves, otters, lynxes and many more.

Unfortunately, Alaska's remoteness deters most Americans from visiting its parks—and their inhabitants. But now the parks are coming to the people, thanks to a series of webcams that in 2012 began broadcasting live feeds from the Brooks River at Katmai National Park and Preserve in Alaska. The stars of the show: brown bears, cousins to the grizzly, who top out at more than 1,000 pounds, thanks in part to their envious diet of fresh salmon. The duel between the fishing bears and the elusive salmon is one of nature's great spectacles, and the park's "bearcams" allow dazzled spectators around the globe to view it in real time during warm-

Virgin Islands N.P. *The island of St. John may hold one key to saving essential coral reefs.*

weather months, when the elusive fish are running.

The cameras at Brooks Falls are carefully positioned: one is located at the top of the falls, a second is just beneath them, and a third (no doubt equipped with a fish-eye lens) offers an underwater view of the salmon doing their best to evade the outreached paws of their predators. Yet as ranger Roy Wood, a 32-year veteran of the NPS, told TIME in February 2016: "We wanted the bearcams to be more than a novelty for viewers along the lines of, 'Hey, I just saw a bear in Alaska catch a fish!' Instead, we wanted to create a virtual campfire, where people around the world could discuss the bears' activities with each other and with those of us who work at the park—and who, in many cases, know each bear's specific habits and behaviors."

> CORAL REEFS HELP FEED HUNDREDS OF MILLIONS OF PEOPLE

Wood laughed when he recalled the park's initial attempts to broadcast the salmon run on the Internet in 2008, which were foiled by the remoteness of the location. But since the Annenberg Foundation's nature outreach program, Explore.org, teamed up with Katmai N.P. to oversee and subsidize the video feed, viewers have flocked to the site (*explore.org/live-cams/player/brown-bear-salmon-cam-brooks-falls*). In 2015, Wood said, the bearcams were watched by 22 million viewers, with many people keeping their feed alive for hours at a time. And four other webcams are now operating at Katmai. That's a mighty big campfire, virtual or not.

Endangered Reefs Far to the south and east of Katmai's fishing bears, rangers and scientists at Virgin Islands N.P. on the island of St. John—a watery world whose environment couldn't be more different from the land of evergreen forests and salmon-filled rivers—are dealing with the effects of climate change. Among the park's wonders are its brilliant coral reefs. But like such reefs around the world, those off the island are suffering from a disease called coral bleaching, in which the living coral communities die off, generally as a result of solar radiation and rising global temperatures. Since the reefs are themselves an ecosystem that sustains marine life, they are essential to the daily diet of millions of people around the world. Scientists estimate that 90% of the planet's coral reefs may be threatened with extinction by 2030.

One possible solution to the problem: discover and cultivate "resilient reefs"—those that can weather the effects of climate change. And in 2014, a team of scientists reported in the journal *Biogeosciences* that they had discovered precisely such reefs at Hurricane Hole on St. John. The reefs, which are part of the Virgin Islands Coral Reef National Monument, survived a case of bleaching in 2010. The scientists, led by ecologist Caroline Rogers of the U.S. Geological Survey, concluded that the reefs were resilient because they were heavily shaded from direct sunlight by mangrove forests, suggesting a new strategy for cultivating more-resilient reefs. The mangroves of St. John remind us that as climate change becomes more pronounced, parks can play a major role in learning to live with an uncertain future.

Snakes in the Grass Climate change is not the only challenge to preserving the parks' unique ecosystems. Rangers at one of the most unusual and irreplaceable natural environments in the world, Florida's Everglades N.P., are dealing with an unusual by-product of modern life: invasive foreign species that threaten the survival of many of the indigenous animal species that make the "River of Grass" such a biological treasure.

The invaders are Burmese pythons, native to Southeast Asia, which began appearing in the Everglades around 2000. It's likely that pythons brought in as pets had either escaped or were released into the wild, and then—like so many other retirees—fell in love with the Sunshine State's climate. Today there may be as many as 100,000 Burmese pythons living amid the wetlands of South Florida, though no one really knows: pythons can disappear when they want to, which is most of the time. During a monthlong hunt in 2013, nearly 1,600 volunteers found and captured only 68 pythons.

Scientists have linked a drastic decline in small mammals in the park to the pythons, which can lay up to 100 eggs at a time and face no natural predators in Florida. "Removing a huge portion of all the mammals from the Everglades is going to have a dramatic impact on the ecosystem," Michael Dorcas, a herpetologist at Davidson College in North Carolina, told TIME's Bryan Walsh in 2014. "But right now we don't have anything that can significantly suppress the python population."

The pythons have proved particularly successful invaders, but they're hardly alone. In the Caribbean, lionfish scour coral reefs of sea life; in the Northeast, emerald ash borers turn trees into kindling; in the Great Lakes, zebra mussels encrust pipes and valves, rendering power plants useless. Add in climate change and the challenge of keeping a balance between humans and the wild, and the message is clear: parks are essential to help us explore, chart and navigate the planet's uncertain future.

Everglades N.P., Florida *From top: the Burmese pythons that have invaded the Everglades generally grow to be 12 feet long. One creature they've battled: the alligators that are the park's iconic animal. At bottom, storks take wing; pythons eat their eggs and threaten their survival in the area.*

Profile: John Muir

Father of Our National Parks

The Whitman of the woods, he made conservation a national priority

JOHN MUIR WAS A "POETICO-TRAMPO-geologist-botanist and ornithologist-naturalist, etc. etc.!!!" That's his description, not ours, and it gives a good sense of a man whose intense bond with the natural world made him a persuasive advocate for the conservation of America's natural treasures. Muir was a visionary who is remembered as the father of our national park system and, as the co-founder and longtime president of the Sierra Club, the creator of the environmental movement. Muir had a pivotal role in the history of the U.S. that is still coming into complete focus: he is slowly taking his place in the pantheon of the nation's greatest visionaries and agents of change. That's our description, not his.

Born in Dunbar, Scotland, in 1838, Muir immigrated to the U.S. with his family in 1849 and settled in Wis-

consin. As a youth, he displayed a natural aptitude for tinkering, experimenting, and creating helpful and ingenious devices. Growing up, he frequently clashed with his stern, religious father, found himself attracted to nature studies and developed a strong wanderlust that stayed with him throughout his life. In his 20s he spent two and a half years at the University of Wisconsin–Madison, where he studied botany, chemistry and geology and was a campus character, known for his inventive genius and lack of concern for social decorum.

In the 1860s Muir, eager to see the world, followed his younger brother to Canada, where he demonstrated his skills as an innovator at an Ontario sawmill and rake and broom factory, then put in a successful stint at an Indianapolis wagon-wheel plant. But when he injured his eye at work in 1867 and was confined to a dark bedroom for a month, the experience made him long to be on the move again. Once recovered, he lit out on a long walking tour to Florida, a trip he recorded in his book *A Thousand-Mile Walk to the Gulf.* As a boy, Muir kept detailed journals of his nature studies; he published a number of books in his lifetime and a wealth of scientific papers and magazine articles, and several more books were published posthumously.

On his journey to Florida, Muir contracted malaria, and he ended up in Cuba, where he explored the tropical flowers for a month. Eventually he booked passage to the promised land he had dreamed of for years: the rugged mountains and wide-open spaces of California. When he arrived in San Francisco in 1868, the wanderer had found a home. He would spend the rest of his life in the Golden State, though his lifelong urge to simply keep moving often drew him into long excursions.

In the first flush of his romance with the West's outsize grandeur, Muir spent a week in Yosemite. His response to its wonders was Whitmanesque—ecstatic, religious, primal—and he soon returned. For the next few years he lived at Yosemite in a series of humble shacks he built by hand, working at a sawmill and as a shepherd. He survived on spare meals, even as he thrived on the spiritual nourishment he felt in the land and in his copy of Ralph Waldo Emerson's essays.

Muir eventually became the presiding spirit of Yosemite, sought out by visitors for his detailed knowledge of its forests and waterfalls, its geology and plants. (He favored flora over fauna and despised grazing animals that devoured flowers and meadow grasses.) When Emerson visited Yosemite in 1871, the two men met, and the Sage of Concord, taken with Muir, offered to obtain a post at Harvard for him. Muir declined, saying, "I never for a moment thought of giving up God's big show for a mere profship!"

With Emerson's imprimatur, Muir blossomed. He spent the next years publishing well-received scientific papers on geology and botany, and he traveled widely. Heeding the advice of friends as he passed 40, the hermit of the woods married the well-to-do Louisa

("Louie") Strentzel, became the father of two daughters, and embarked on a more settled life in Martinez, Calif., where he managed his father-in-law's orchards. But his conversion was not complete; Louisa knew her husband well enough to "shoo him" out of the house now and then for a journey to his beloved forests or, later, abroad.

As he engaged more with civilization and less with trees, Muir became a charismatic advocate for the preservation of the nation's natural resources, then as now seen by some business interests as sources of wealth rather than spiritual inspiration. Muir argued that only federal protection could preserve the great spaces of the West from his personal demon, development. His powerful sermon: "Through all the wonderful, eventful centuries . . . God has cared for these trees, saved them from drought, disease, avalanches, and a thousand straining, leveling tempests and floods; but he cannot save them from fools—only Uncle Sam can do that."

Muir scored a victory when Congress approved the protection of Yosemite in 1890. His work as an advocate led to his co-founding of the Sierra Club in 1892; the group became a strong voice for preservation. But even Muir couldn't win his long battle to stop the damming of Yosemite's Tuolumne River, which ran through its Hetch Hetchy Valley, to create a reservoir for San Francisco, especially in the wake of the fires that devastated the city after the earthquake of 1906. Muir died in 1914, the year after the dam was approved—and two years before the creation of the federal agency he long supported but did not live to see, the National Park Service.

Theodore Roosevelt, center, visited Yosemite with Muir, fourth from right, in 1903. The two became allies, giving Muir critical political support in Washington.

Redwood N.P., California
Novelist John Steinbeck declared, "The redwoods, once seen, leave a mark or create a vision that stays with you always."

Going to Extremes

The national parks are the
habitats of nature's superlatives

TREES THAT SOAR HIGH INTO THE SKY and live for millennia. Deep lakes that crown volcanic mountaintops. Vast glaciers and ice fields, blazing deserts that are cauldrons of heat, and subterranean chambers that stretch for hundreds of miles. America's 59 national parks not only preserve the nation's most beautiful and important ecosystems, they also capture nature in its most extreme forms.

Mark Twain declared that "there are three kinds of lies: lies, damned lies—and statistics." But the statistics we have relied upon to measure the geological and climatic extremes to be found in our national parks are accurate, and they paint a compelling picture of the immensity and variety of the American landscape.

Giants of the Forest Imagine a living organism that stretches horizontally almost one third longer than a football field. Now imagine hoisting it into a vertical position so it rises more than 30 stories into the sky. That's one way to envision the sheer immensity of the mighty redwood trees that are protected in several national parks in California, including Redwood, Yosemite, Sequoia and Kings Canyon. The U.S. is home to two of the three known species of these green Goliaths.

The redwoods in the groves preserved in eastern California's Sierra Nevada range are known to scientists as *Sequoiadendron giganteum* (giant sequoia), and they are *giganteum* indeed. But they aren't even the tallest trees in the National Park system; they can't measure up to the *Sequoia sempervirens*, coastal redwoods that flourish in the perpetually damp environment of the temperate rain forest along California's northern Pacific coast. That's where you can find the loftiest known tree in the U.S.—and on the planet—the Hyperion tree, which is

Kings Canyon N.P., California *Long droughts were a cause of wildfires that devastated large swaths of the park in 2015.*

preserved within Redwood N.P. At 379 feet, it's 85 feet taller than Yosemite's tallest sequoia, the Columbia.

The Hyperion is a relative newcomer to the title of world's tallest tree. Its height was determined in 2006, when a group of forest scientists established its height the old-fashioned way—by scaling it and unfurling a tape measure from its very top to the forest floor.

John Steinbeck once called the redwoods "ambassadors from another time"; they can live for thousands of years. The General Sherman in Sequoia National Park is 2,300 to 2,700 years old. Sadly, drought-fed wildfires raged through many of California's national parks in 2015, including Kings Canyon, Sequoia and Yosemite.

But when it comes to extreme longevity, the sequoias live only half as long as some of the longest-living trees on earth, the Great Basin bristlecone pines, *Pinus longaeva*, that can be found in Inyo National Forest amid the White

Mammoth Cave N.P., Kentucky *The caverns formed ages ago when water dissolved limestone rock deposits.*

Mountains of the eastern Sierras. Here dwells Methuselah, a gnarly, twisted bristlecone pine that is estimated by the U.S. Forest Service to be more than 4,000 years old.

Depths amid the Heights Looking for the deepest lake in the U.S.? Then start climbing, for it's located in the most unlikely of places—more than 6,000 feet above sea level, high amid Oregon's Cascade Range. Crater Lake National Park is one of the most unique geological features on the planet: a vast, roughly circular lake between five and six miles in diameter, it is nestled in the caldera formed when volcanic Mount Mazama erupted some 7,700 years ago. The blast was so powerful that it reduced the size of the mountain, estimated to be more than 12,000 feet at the time, by thousands of feet.

Crater Lake is a sparkling, ethereal blue, and it resembles a goblet into which wine is poured, for it is not fed by rivers and streams; rather, it is renewed by rain and snow. Its waters stretch 1,949 feet down into the cavity formed when the mountain blew its top, and they are among the clearest to be found on the planet. Within the lake is Wizard Island, an example of a cinder cone built up by smaller eruptions in the hundreds of years after Mazama's big blast. It rises some 2,700 feet from the floor of the caldera, poking its top about 763 feet above the lake level. In a nifty example of natural forces in

Crater Lake N.P., Oregon *Wizard Island, within Crater Lake's caldera, boasts a caldera of its own at its summit.*

action, Wizard Island itself is topped by a small volcanic caldera, composing a sort of geological matryoshka doll. In summer months, park visitors can take boat rides to the island and explore its mini-mountain, cradled within the walls that surround Crater Lake

Underground Wonders Mammoth Cave National Park in south-central Kentucky is one of the planet's great treasures: with its labyrinthine passages stretching for 405 miles, it is by far the longest known cave system on earth. Long explored by Native Americans, the cave became known to white settlers in the late 1790s, and it was mined during the War of 1812, when British blockades of U.S. coasts made salt a desirable commodity and the cave's saltpeter reserves became highly valuable.

Through the 19th century, the cave became an increasingly popular tourist attraction, amid growing concerns that its use by private companies was harming its natural wonders. Like Niagara Falls, it demonstrated how unchecked consumer interests can turn a natural wonder into an unnatural blunder. African-American slave Stephen Bishop guided tourists through the caverns for two decades and was the first to explore, chart and name many of the system's best-known features. But it was not until 1941 that the complex, consisting of both the underground passages and some 52,830 acres of the forested lands above, was absorbed into the National Park system.

> MAMMOTH CAVE KEEPS GROWING, AS LENGTHY NEW PASSAGEWAYS ARE FOUND

The cave system began forming some 10 million years ago, geologists believe, and the official measured length of Mammoth Cave keeps expanding, primarily because of the ongoing discovery of new passageways within the vast complex by NPS speleologists and volunteers, who say "there is no end in sight" to the cave's extent.

Water in Motion The tallest waterfall in the nation— and in the national parks—is Yosemite Falls in California, whose vertical drop measures 2,425 feet, about 200 feet short of a half-mile. In contrast, the tallest of the three waterfalls that make up Niagara Falls, American Falls, is a mere 180 feet tall. The cascade is composed of three segments: Upper Yosemite Fall (1,430 feet), the middle cascades (675 feet) and Lower Yosemite Fall (320 feet). Its waters consist primarily of snowmelt from the mountains: it is a seasonal phenomenon. Visitors to the park in

Yosemite N.P., California *Brimming with water in this photograph, the flow of Yosemite Falls has fallen victim to drought in recent years.*

Wrangell–St. Elias N.P., Alaska *Snowmelt on the Root Glacier gathers in a blue pool of matchless clarity. The enormous ice fields and glaciers in Alaska's national parks are receding rapidly in size as global temperatures rise.*

early summer are treated to the sight of the falls at their gushing peak. But by August, visitors may find the water has slowed to a trickle or even stopped completely before autumn rains jump-start the flow again.

Or so went the annual cycle at Yosemite, since this magnificent realm of natural beauty was first set aside for preservation by Congress and President Abraham Lincoln in 1864. But in recent years, Yosemite, like the rest of California, has suffered from scant rainfall. Yes, exceptions occur: in 2011 the Associated Press reported, "Record Sierra snowfall over the winter now means record snowmelt as temperatures rise, swelling Yosemite National Park's iconic waterfalls, streams and rivers to their most turbulent level in years. Yosemite Falls, the nation's tallest, is spewing enough water to fill a gasoline tanker truck every two seconds."

But a long, tenacious drought struck California in 2012, and by March 28, 2015, a *Los Angeles Times* headline declared, IN STORE FOR YOSEMITE VISITORS: A DRIER, BROWNER PARK. The article, by Louis Sahagun, reported: "Yosemite National Park is bracing for its driest year on record. Yosemite Falls will probably go dry

> ALASKA'S VOLCANOES ARE PERCHED ON THE PACIFIC "RING OF FIRE"

in June." And it did. As the planet heats up, dealing with climate change has become one of the most urgent of the diverse challenges that face the NPS.

A Vast, Wild Kingdom The single largest holding in the parks system is Wrangell–St. Elias National Park and Preserve in southern Alaska. At 13.2 million acres, it is so large that the NPS conveys its size by comparison, noting that the park and preserve are the size of Yellowstone and Yosemite put together—with the nation of Switzerland thrown in for good measure.

This immense region is so remote that it attracts fewer than 75,000 visitors a year. Yet it holds a cornucopia of geological wonders, including Mount St. Elias, at 18,008 feet above sea level the second-highest peak in the U.S., after Denali, also in Alaska. Mount Wrangell, named for Alaska's Russian governor in the years before the U.S. purchased the present state in 1867, rises to 14,163 feet. Perched on the northeast corner of the Ring of Fire, the region of tectonic activity that encircles the Pacific Ocean basin, Wrangell is an active volcano, with a large caldera filling its broad summit.

Its most recent activity dates to 1902—only yesterday, as geologists measure time.

Wrangell–St. Elias is also home to the largest glacial system in North America. In recent years the glaciers have been shrinking, another sign of the heating trend across the planet. The national park is also one of North America's largest wildlife preserves, where mammals roam, from caribou, elk, bear and gray wolves to wolverines and foxes. Cold-weather birds are plentiful, and the rivers teem with trout, pike and the pricey salmon from the Copper River that are highly esteemed by gourmets.

The Bottom Line California is a land of extremes, home to not only the tallest living things in the U.S., the soaring sequoia trees, but also to Death Valley, the unique desert habitat that is the lowest, hottest and driest place in North America. How low? At its deepest point, the 5,270 square miles of the valley are 282 feet below sea level. How hot? The valley's Furnace Creek holds the record for the highest reliably recorded air temperature ever taken on the planet's surface: 134°F, on July 10, 1913. How dry? In three specific years—1929, 1953 and 1989—meteorologists recorded that the desert valley received zero rainfall for the entire year.

The average annual precipitation in Death Valley is less than two inches. Yet when the rains do fall, the valley floor can burst into life, with wildflowers blooming in a place named for death by 19th-century prospectors. One such "superbloom" occured in February 2016, when El Niño weather patterns and heavy October rainfall nourished the soil just enough to invite millions of seedlings that had been lying dormant for as long as a decade to the surface for the first time since 2005, covering the desert floor with a stunning carpet of yellow blossoms.

In a system of national parks that celebrates some of the most bountiful regions on the planet, Death Valley reminds visitors that nature has a bias toward life, even amid the harshest of environments.

Death Valley N.P., California *Forecast: hot and dry. A tourist takes a selfie on the planet's lowest patch of ground.*

President Roosevelt strikes a pose on his visit to Yosemite in 1903, when he spent a night camping with early national park advocate John Muir.

Profile: Theodore Roosevelt

A President with a Passion for Nature

Who speaks for the forests? A cowboy from downtown Manhattan

MARK HANNA WAS THE FOREMOST power broker in the Republican Party in the 1890s, and he exerted all his skills to help his protégé, William McKinley, win the 1896 presidential election. Four years later, Hanna controlled every aspect of McKinley's re-election campaign except one: he was forced to accept as the president's running mate the unvarnished, unpredictable and notoriously unmanageable hero of the Spanish-American War, Theodore Roosevelt. McKinley and Roosevelt won the election—but McKinley was assassinated after he been in office only six months into his second term. When Hanna heard the news, he bemoaned the turn of events, declaring, "Now that damned cowboy is president of the United States!"

Yes, he was—and a highly unlikely cowboy at that.

Born into a wealthy and well-connected New York City family in 1858, Roosevelt was raised to take his place among Manhattan's elites. But from early in his youth, "Teedie" displayed a fascination with the natural world and the sciences of botany and zoology that set him apart from his peers. At the age of 12, he was the proprietor, curator, lecturer and field representative of the "Roosevelt Natural History Museum." Its holdings: some 1,000 specimens of plants and animals collected by hand. Its location: Master Roosevelt's bedroom.

Roosevelt was sickly and weak as a child, but he vowed to make himself strong, and he kept that vow. Never more himself than when he was outdoors, he loved nature, knew the songs of dozens of birds, and loved to ride, climb, hike and shoot. As a political progressive, he became a reformer who sought to whip society into shape, just as he had driven himself into robust masculinity. At age 23, he was elected to the New York State Assembly and embarked on a political career as a progressive Republican.

Roosevelt's life took an abrupt detour when the rising politician, only 25, was afflicted by a ghastly tragedy: his wife, Alice, died two days after giving birth to a daughter. Earlier on the same day, Roosevelt's mother, Martha, had also passed away. With his spirit crushed, Roosevelt turned his back on his political career and followed a boyhood dream: the young man went West.

Roosevelt had visited the Dakota Territory in 1883 and had learned to love its wide-open spaces. Now he made his home on the range, and in the years that followed, the patrician turned himself into a true cowboy. In the rough hill country, his love of nature blossomed as never before—and he also saw, firsthand, the debilitating effects of heedless exploitation of resources. Only two decades before, the Dakota plains had swarmed with bison, but by the late 1880s, the organized slaughter of them, mainly to feed railroad-building crews, left fewer than 500 bison alive across the Great Plains.

Roosevelt returned to New York, married for a second time, and—after losing half his Dakota cattle herd in the frigid winter of 1886–'87—he resumed his career as a crusader for progressive political reforms. He served very capably as chief of the U.S. Civil Service Commission, then became an energetic and effective police commissioner in New York City. In 1897 he was named assistant secretary of the Navy by President William McKinley. Taking advantage of a four-hour stint as acting secretary, he managed to jump-start the Spanish-American War. He then recruited a wild cadre of Western cowpokes and Harvard friends to form the Rough Riders—and made himself the hero of the war he started, leading his band of irregulars on their victorious charge up San Juan Hill in Cuba.

It was that charge that carried Roosevelt, at full gallop, onto McKinley's ticket—and by 1901, the "damned cowboy" was president. Once in office, "T.R.," only 42, channeled his passion for nature into his activist executive agenda, launching policies designed to defend America's natural treasures and becoming the first U.S. president to fully embrace the cause of conservation.

In 1903 Roosevelt visited Yosemite, where he hobnobbed with the high priest of the conservation movement, John Muir, who convinced him that the federal government, not the states, must be mobilized to preserve the nation's natural wonders and resources. Roosevelt agreed, creating the U.S. Forest Service and finding the right man to lead the new agency: lumber scion Gifford Pinchot, who helped impose strict federal controls over commercial use of woodlands.

The year after he left the White House, Roosevelt explained his philosophy to an audience in Kansas. He recognized the right, he said, even the "duty," of his generation to use the nation's natural resources. "But I do not recognize the right to waste them," he added. "Or to rob, by wasteful use, the generations that come after us."

Practicing what he preached, Roosevelt set aside immense tracts of land for future generations: 150 National Forests, 51 Federal Bird Reservations, five National Parks, 18 National Monuments, four National Game Preserves and more. In all, he placed under federal protection nearly 230 million acres. By the time he was done, the damned cowboy had earned himself a place on Mount Rushmore, in his old Dakota home. It makes a bully perch for the president who put the husbandry of the environment on the nation's political map for the first time.

Roosevelt loved nothing more than roughing it out West; his cowboy persona was earned, not a political pose. "Let us live in the harness, striving mightily," he once declared. Above, he's in the saddle, at right, in 1905.

National Park of American Samoa
Welcome to the only U.S. national park located below the equator.

Far Away in
Space and Time

The park system stretches to exotic ports of call—
and transports us centuries back in history

TROPICAL RAIN FORESTS CLOAKING steep volcanic hillsides in a sea of green. Vibrant coral reefs, home to octopus and sharks. Humpback whales breaching and spouting as they pass through on their annual migrations through the vast Pacific Ocean. Yes, we're enjoying the amenities of a U.S. national park, but it's clear we're not in Yosemite anymore—or Acadia or Olympic or Zion. We're not even in Hawaii, home to the other tropical-weather parks of the Pacific. Instead, we're in the National Park of American Samoa, the only national park located below the equator. It's one of the far-flung parks—in both space and time—we'll visit in this chapter, which highlights the sheer reach of the properties administered by the National Park Service.

Pacific Paradise Authorized in 1988, the N.P. of American Samoa is one of the newer national parks, and it is steadily succeeding in its founding mission: to preserve the tropical environment of these remote islands in the mid-Pacific, some 2,600 miles southwest of Hawaii, and to encourage visitors to experience their wonders.

American Samoa consists of five volcanic islands, Tutuila, Aunu'u, Ofu, Olosega, Ta'u; and two distant atolls, Rose Atoll and Swains Island. Its companion is the independent state of Samoa, formerly known as Western Samoa, a much larger island chain that achieved independence from New Zealand in 1962.

American Samoa is an unincorporated territory of the U.S. and has been under U.S. protection since 1900, after the nation became involved in the Pacific in the 1890s, during a short-lived period of American colonialism in the region. Samoans are famously proud of their ties to

the U.S.; the islands boast the highest rate of military enlistment of any U.S. state or territory.

The national park consists of three separate sections: the largest and most popular of them is located on the main island of Tutuila, near the harbor city of Pago Pago; smaller parks are located on Ofu and Ta'u. A visit to Tutuila is not for tenderfeet, as the primary attraction is hiking the ridge lines through the volcanic island's forested slopes to discover its rich diversity of plants and animals. Snorkeling and scuba diving are popular, particularly on Ofu, which is celebrated for its spectacular coral reefs.

History buffs will want to hike the mountain trails around Pago Pago to recall the days when war reached these peaceful islands. After the Japanese attack on Pearl Harbor in 1941, American Samoa became an important part of the chain of islands controlled by the enemies of the Japanese Empire. Protective U.S. artillery emplacements can still be seen on the hillside trails, even though the only Japanese attack on the island occurred early in the war, on Jan. 11, 1942, when a submarine fired on the U.S. Naval Base in Pago Pago Harbor, but failed to do serious damage.

Mother Nature, however, scored a direct hit on American Samoa on Sept. 29, 2009, when the islands were rocked by a major earthquake, with Pago Pago, as well as the national park, suffering extensive damage. But the park has largely recovered from the quake, which registered 8.0 magnitude on the Richter scale. The quake was followed by devastating tsunami waves, but NPS authorities say the park has recovered from the natural disaster.

The Lure of Lava The N.P. of American Samoa is the most remote of the U.S. national parks, but it is not the only park located on a volcanic island in the Pacific. Ha-

> A DEVASTATING
> EARTHQUAKE
> ROCKED THE
> SAMOAS IN
> 2009

Hawaii Volcanoes N.P. *On Kilauea the spectacle of incandescent lava meeting the sea is a daily occurrence.*

waii Volcanoes N.P. was established in 1916, and thus the park will celebrate its centennial year in tandem with the NPS. Located on the island of Hawaii, the park is home to two volcanoes: Kilauea, one of the most active volcanoes on the planet, and Mauna Loa, the largest active volcano on earth. In 2014, 1.6 million visitors traveled to the park to marvel at them.

Kilauea is the Old Faithful of volcanoes; its name roughly translates as "spewing" in Hawaiian, and it has been in a constant state of gentle eruption since 1983, thrilling visitors as its lava streams cascade into the Pacific, sending plumes of smoke aloft in one of the planet's great, hissing encounters of fire and water.

> MOST OF MAUNA LOA'S SURFACE IS COVERED BY THE WAVES

Mauna Loa is far less active than Kilauea; its last major eruption was in 1984. Even though the vast mountain makes up more than half the surface area of the island of Hawaii, it is even more massive than it appears, for much of its bulk lies beneath the surface of the Pacific. Seen from above the ground, Kilauea is taller than Mauna Loa by some 200 feet. But measured from the ocean's floor, Mauna Loa is the tallest "mountain" on the planet: topping 30,000 feet from its base on the bottom of the Pacific to its summit, Mauna Loa is even taller than Mount Everest.

The unique activity of Kilauea, particularly the predictable gentleness of its lava flow, has attracted geologists as well as tourists. The Hawaii Volcano Observatory, founded in 1912, continues to monitor seismic activity in the islands and is regarded as one of the most important centers of volcanology on the planet. Located within the grounds of the national park, it is perched on the caldera of Kilauea, offering visitors a spectacular view of the incandescent, lava-filled crater.

A Journey into the Past Some of our national parks are far away in time rather than space. Mesa Verde N.P. in Colorado is one of the most striking of them. The park consists of more than 50,000 acres in the Four Corners area of the Southwest, where Utah, Colorado, Arizona and New Mexico come together. Signs of human habitation here date back to 7500 B.C., when nomadic Paleo-Indians roamed the area. But the major attractions of the park for today's tourists are the spectacular cliff dwellings created in much more recent centuries by the Ancestral Puebloan peoples, whose culture took shape around A.D. 400 to 750, enjoyed a Classical Period that began in 1100, and then, around 1300, abruptly disappeared.

Taking advantage of advances in basket-weaving and agriculture, the early Puebloan people abandoned the nomadic ways of their ancestors and began living in a new type of dwelling, the pueblo, which featured interconnected, many-chambered buildings made of sandstone blocks and mud mortar, in which many families lived. These communities were built into the rugged cliff faces of the region, using rock formations to provide shelter. Unlike their ancestors, the Puebloans lived year-round in their dwellings, forming self-contained communities. They also gathered in shallow pits, or kivas, they dug into the ground, although scientists have not reached a consensus on the nature and purpose of these assemblies.

The most remarkable of the Puebloan dwellings is the largest of them, the famous Cliff Palace in southwestern Colorado. This complex apparently reached its peak around 1260, when it is thought to have accommodated

> **THE PUEBLOAN PEOPLE ABRUPTLY ABANDONED THEIR HOMES**

some 100 residents in 150 rooms. The community also included more than 20 kivas, with the largest of them at the center of the elaborate communal structure.

The Cliff Palace is located in a horizontal gash that runs across a steep cliff face, a highly defensible position. Scientists conjecture that it may have been a central administrative structure for the surrounding region; its title as a palace reflects that opinion. But its glory days were brief: by 1300 it was deserted. Scholars posit that a long series of droughts led to warfare among the various tribes in the region and the eventual abandonment of this Shangri-la of the Southwest.

Mesa Verde is only one of the many far-flung parks, memorials and monuments that preserve America's past. Dry Tortugas N.P., located off the southernmost coast of Florida, 70 miles west of Key West, combines the tropical ecology of Hawaii and American Samoa with the historic grandeur of Mesa Verde. The park consists of about 64,000 acres, the vast majority of which is underwater, and it draws avid snorkelers and divers, as well as flocks of birdwatchers. Seven islands

Mesa Verde N.P., Colorado *The Cliff Palace was discovered in 1888 by two cowboys looking for stray cattle.*

dot the sea; the largest of them is home to Fort Jefferson, a 19th-century edifice that was built to protect the naturally deep anchorage in the Dry Tortugas from enemy control. Though never completed, the huge building still holds the distinction of being the largest masonry building in the Americas, and it remains a fascinating artifact of naval and political strategy in the 1800s.

Peak Experience A vertical wonder tops off this survey of some of the most distant and ancient of our national parks. At 20,310 feet, the summit of Mount Denali in Alaska is not only the highest point in the national park system, it's also the loftiest perch in North America. Each year, about 1,000 hardy mountaineers set out to reach its summit, but it's a demanding trek, and only some 50% of them reach the top and return bearing the selfies to prove they succeeded.

Denali National Park—known as Mount McKinley before its Native American name was restored in August 2015—offers far more to explore across its 6-million-acre expanse than its ever-snowy peak. Like so many of the first national parks, Denali is bound up with the presidency of Theodore Roosevelt, who heard about the area's abundant resources and rugged beauty from his friend Charles Sheldon, an ardent conservationist whose account of his adventures in the area in 1906-'08, *The Wilderness of Denali*, was published posthumously in 1930.

> DENALI N.P. HELPED SAVE THE GRAY WOLF FROM EXTINCTION

Sheldon was particularly alarmed by the slaughter of local wildlife by market hunters to feed prospectors, who flooded the area after gold was discovered there in 1903. The impetus that drove the creation of Denali as a national park in 1917 was as much a desire to preserve Alaska's wildlife from over-hunting, the curse that almost led to the extinction of the Great Plains bison, as to protect its natural beauty.

Beginning in 1939, Denali paid off on that vision, as NPS wildlife biologist Adolph Murie studied the behavior of Denali's gray wolves and helped save the predator at a time when the wolves had been almost eliminated in today's Lower 48 states. Murie also firmly opposed plans that would have made the park more accessible, helping restrict vehicular traffic into the park and thus ensuring that Denali would remain wild long into the future.

These radically different parks, stretching across vast swaths of the globe, preserving the past as well as the present, and guarding volcanoes, wildlife, tropical reefs and subpolar regions, help constitute an enormous, peaceable kingdom devoted to conserving our planet.

Enduring Portraits of Primal Forces

The visual chronicler of the parks didn't take pictures—he made them

ANSEL ADAMS WAS THE POET OF THE gray spectrum, the man who dipped the American sublime into the inkpot of black-and-white photography and by that means made it new again," TIME critic Richard Lacayo wrote in a review of a 2009 exhibit of Adams's photographs. "So persuasive were his methods that because of him we tend to think of the national parks the way we think of the Great Depression, as something we can barely conceive of in color. He almost made us believe that the whole of creation comes in the palette of a cinder block—and to be glad about it."

Adams was born in 1902 in San Francisco. The son of an insurance executive, he was raised in a chalet-like house overlooking the Golden Gate. He learned to play the piano under the stern tutelage of a German music instructor, who taught him, he later said, the necessity of technical excellence in the pursuit of artistic expression. His favorite composers are no surprise, given his photographs. "I've always liked heroic music," he told TIME's late art critic Robert Hughes in 1979. "I can't stand Debussy and Ravel. I like Beethoven, Bach, Chopin, Scriabin—anything architectural and big has much more appeal to me."

In 1916 Adams took along a Kodak Brownie on his first trip to Yosemite Valley, and what he saw through that lens—something architectural and big— awakened him. The mountains gave him both subject and occupation: as a youth he took a caretaker's job at Yosemite for the Sierra Club. Later, he would sit for 37 years on the board of the club co-founded by John Muir and become an unflagging champion of environmental protection.

Like Muir, Adams looked to Ralph Waldo Emerson as his North Star. Eerie similarities between them coalesce around Yosemite. Like Muir's, Adams's first trip was "a tremendous event," he told Hughes. From that moment, the Sierras—"that great earth gesture"—dominated his life. He was married there, to fellow Californian Virginia Best; one of his two children was born there; and for some six decades he made an annual pilgrimage to marvel at its wonders—the hajj that refreshes.

Adams's early photographs were influenced by the soft-focus pictorial tradition in which the image was retouched to make it more painterly. In 1930 he met fellow cameraman Paul Strand, whose style was crisp, straight, unfussed. Recalled Adams, "I came home

At left, Adams's photo Moon and Half Dome *was shot in 1960 in the park that most inspired both Adams and John Muir: Yosemite. Above, Adams shows off both his big Kodak Brownie and big smile near his home in Carmel, Calif., in 1981.*

Adams's large-format photos, like Tetons and Snake River *(1942), carry a huge amount of what he called "information."*

thinking, 'Now photography exists!'" His new direction was fixed, and his success launched by the dean of American photography at the time, Alfred Stieglitz, who in 1936 gave Adams his first one-man show in New York. Adams built on his growing fame throughout the 1930s with exhibits on the West Coast; commercial assignments, including shoots for *Life* and *Fortune*; and how-to books for young photographers.

In 1941 Adams was given a dream commission: he was hired by the Department of the Interior to shoot national parks, Native American sites and other historic locations to decorate the department's Washington offices. Guggenheim fellowships in 1946 and '48 allowed him to shoot every national park. Thus, for several years, Adams lugged his old-school, large-format view camera from park to park, taking the photographs that are his foremost achievement. The heavy camera rested on a tripod and required the operator to duck under a black

cloth, shooting in a manner not unlike that of Mathew Brady's corps of cameramen in the Civil War.

Late in 2015, as part of the National Park Service's celebration of its 2016 centennial, the Department of the Interior announced that it would seek a photographer to hold the same position Adams held in the 1940s. The full-time job will be based in Washington, with the photographer asked to shoot large-format documentary photos for the Library of Congress and create presentations about them for the public. The reaction was large, and the lucky applicant is expected to be named in the early summer of 2016.

Adams's shoes will be hard to fill, for his sensitivity to nature was backed up by supreme technical knowledge and control. To him, a negative was not just the record of a moment but "the source of the information required for the creation of the print." His prints are surprisingly small. To achieve the utmost sharpness, some were produced as contact prints from the large pieces of film he used in his trademark camera.

Adams's uncompromising craftsmanship helped pioneer the public recognition of photography as an art form. His method was to control rigorously every element of the picture: lighting, composition, focus. The image for him broke down into 10 distinct "zones" of tonal quality, ranging from deepest black to pure white, a careful symmetry of light and dark. "The negative is the score," he said. "The print is the performance."

By the mid-'60s, Adams had virtually ceased taking new photographs, concentrating instead on making prints of earlier works (the performance grew darker and moodier) and updating his 40 books on photography, as his pictures rose steadily in price. Bluff and leprechaun-like, Adams in his later years became a peripatetic, much-loved public figure, the gnome of Half Dome, and his familiar works suffered, ironically enough, from overexposure.

Artistically, the photographer's popularity reflected the fact that his classic 19th-century style possessed more than a trace of romanticism. "People look at my pictures," he said, "and then accept them, in a sense, as reality." But instead it was the heightened reality of a photographer who made nature seem like Nature, as TIME's Richard Stengel observed in the magazine's obituary after Adams died at 82 in 1984.

"You don't take a photograph; you make it," Adams once said. He made himself into a photographer and then made others see the world through his eyes. The result of his work was not an instant captured in time but timelessness captured forever in an instant.

Adams took Jeffrey Pine, Sentinel Dome *(1940) at Yosemite in 1940. The 400-year-old tree collapsed in 2003.*

Preserving America's Heritage

"... the President of the United States is hereby authorized ... to declare by public proclamation historic landmarks, historic and prehistoric structures, and other objects of historic or scientific interest ... to be national monuments ...**"**

—TEXT, THE ANTIQUITIES ACT OF 1906
Legislation that authorized the president to name National Monuments

Martin Luther King Jr. Memorial, Washington
Dedicated on Oct. 16, 2011, the statue on the National Mall was created by sculptor Yei Lixin.

A Nation of Gateways

Indelible monuments celebrate the heritage of an ever-changing nation

Statue of Liberty National Monument, New York *The statue itself is 151 feet tall from base to torch, but it rises to a height of 305 feet, thanks to its 89-foot pedestal and 65-foot star-shaped base.*

T HE LIFE OF A STATUE MIGHT SEEM A bit predictable, one day much like the next. But for the Statue of Liberty, the towering edifice that stands sentinel in New York Harbor as a symbol of America's founding principles and its heritage as a land of immigrants, the past three decades have been uncharacteristically eventful. The ravages of time, the predations of terrorists and the brute force of Mother Nature have unleashed a series of afflictions on one of the most recognized monuments on the planet. Yet the beloved statue endures, each cycle of setback and restoration making it more accessible to visitors and more meaningful to Americans.

Lady Liberty is only one of the irreplaceable U.S. monuments and memorials maintained by the National Park Service. Many of the great memorials of Washington—including the Lincoln and Jefferson memorials and the Washington Monument—are under NPS jurisdiction. So are scores of hallowed national battlefields, including Gettysburg, Antietam and other major battlegrounds of the Civil War. Hundreds more national historic landmarks honor the nation's heritage and culture, from the Revolutionary War and the Trail of Tears to World War II and the civil rights movement.

As a nation of immigrants who explored and settled a landmass that stretches across a continent, the U.S. has been a gateway to the world, a nation so large it includes interior gateways of its own. In this chapter, we'll explore four national monuments that capture America's international and continental destiny.

A Nation's Beacon The Statue of Liberty holds a special place in American hearts, perhaps because, ironically enough, it was not made in the U.S. Rather, the colossus was a gift to Americans from France, created to honor the two nations' commitment to their shared vision of liberty and equality. As a tribute from outsiders, rather than a homegrown boast, it is all the more meaningful.

The statue was intended to be erected in New York Harbor in 1876 on the centennial of the American Declaration of Independence. But fund-raising campaigns, massive building projects and government bureaucracies being what they have always been, President Grover Cleveland formally dedicated the statue 10 years late, on Oct. 28, 1886, unveiling a French flag that covered

Ellis Island, New York City *Tourists take in the Main Arrivals Hall in Ellis Island's Main Building.*

the face of the copper-clad statue for the ceremony. The work was designed by sculptor Frédéric-Auguste Bartholdi, and its interior bracing was created by Gustave Eiffel, later to win enduring fame for his cast-iron spire in Paris. The torch in the right hand of the colossus, whose formal name is *Liberty Enlightening the World*, was illuminated for the first time three days later, on November 1.

The statue's association with America's immigrants began to take shape even before it was dedicated, when New York poet Emma Lazarus wrote a sonnet, "The New Colossus," which was auctioned at a benefit gala in 1883 to raise money for the construction of a pedestal for the statue. Its ringing description of the statue as a symbol of sanctuary for the "huddled masses yearning to breathe free" is enshrined in the nation's memory.

In 1892, six years after the statue was dedicated, its association with immigration became even stronger, when federal authorities created a processing center for immigrants on nearby Ellis Island in New York Harbor. The statue was declared a national monument in 1924 and was entrusted to the NPS in 1933. Ellis Island was closed as an immigration center in 1954; 11 years later, it was declared part of the Statue of Liberty National Monument and placed in the custody of the park service.

Lady Liberty's Travails The Statue of Liberty presided peacefully over New York Harbor, welcoming 12 million immigrants to nearby Ellis Island between 1892 and 1954, as well as millions of homecoming veterans after the two world wars in Europe. On July 30, 1916, in an in-

Youngsters take the measure of an American flag composed of the faces of former immigrants, now citizens, on Ellis Island.

The buildings on the island were designed in Renaissance Revival style by Edward L. Tilton and William A. Boring.

cident now largely forgotten, the statue was damaged by a series of bomb blasts set off by agents of Imperial Germany on nearby Black Tom Island, site of a major storehouse used by East Coast munitions manufacturers.

The explosions killed several people, injured dozens more and was heard as far away as Philadelphia. The statue sustained nicks from shrapnel and rivets popped on its raised right arm, which had been open to visitors since 1886. Officials quickly restricted public access to the torch, and it has remained closed ever since.

Lady Liberty's next decades were uneventful. But by 1982, as its centennial approached, NPS leaders and others realized that the colossus was in dire need of a structural overhaul after 96 years of service. A new organization, the Statue of Liberty–Ellis Island Foundation, was created to raise funds to restore the structure, and President Ronald Reagan appointed Chrysler Corp. CEO Lee Iacocca, the son of Italian immigrants, to lead the effort.

This time around, the work was completed on time: on July 4, 1986, the renovated statue was rededicated in the climax of a celebratory weekend that was over-the-top, 1980s-style. President Reagan and his wife, Nancy, presided over the ceremonies, which included

12 MILLION IMMIGRANTS PASSED THROUGH ELLIS ISLAND

such pomp and circumstance as a nautical parade in the harbor by 22 historic tall sailing ships, concerts by the Boston Pops and the New York Philharmonic, a gigantic fireworks display and, yes, a blimp race.

Lady Liberty seemed set to lift her lamp beside the golden door for another 100 years, but only 15 years after its renovation, the statue was shut down, amid national mourning and fear, after the terrorist attacks of Sept. 11, 2001, brought down the Twin Towers of the World Trade Center in lower Manhattan, a familiar backdrop to thousands of photos of the statue. Amid concerns of further terrorist strikes, access to Liberty Island was restricted. That ban was lifted 100 days after the attacks, but the base of the statue was closed to the public until 2004, and it wasn't until July 4, 2009, that visitors could once again climb to its spiked crown.

Two years later, the interior of the statue was again shut down, as part of a renovation designed to increase traffic flow in its interior. The $30 million, three-year makeover made the climb to the crown a bit less arduous for visitors, increasing the number of steps required, from 354 to 393, but shortening the height of each step.

On Oct. 28, 2012, New Yorkers and the nation cheered the reopening of the statue on schedule. But

**Jefferson National Expansion
Memorial, Missouri** *The Gateway Arch
is currently separated from downtown St.
Louis—but not for much longer.*

the day after those long-awaited festivities, Hurricane Sandy crashed into the New York area. The storm surge left both Liberty Island and Ellis Island largely underwater and destroyed much of the infrastructure on both islands, including the piers that allowed ferry access to them. Once again the Statue of Liberty was shut down, but this time her comeback was swift: on July 4, 2013, both Lady Liberty and Ellis Island were back on duty.

For Ellis Island, that's a lot of duty. In the years after 1954, when the facility was closed by federal immigration authorities, it fell into disrepair. As the NPS admits, "The silent and empty immigration depot rapidly deteriorated into a ghostly complex of dilapidated buildings."

The restoration of Ellis Island was one of the major goals of the centennial campaign, and the Ellis Island Immigration Museum opened in 1990 in the restored Main Arrivals Hall. As other facilities on the island have been restored to their original appearance, the complex has become a powerful attraction for tourists. In 2015 the museum's exhibit space was further expanded when the new Peopling of America Center opened, and the museum's name was changed to the Ellis Island National Museum of Immigration. More than 3 million visitors journey to Ellis Island each year, many of them members of the 40% of Americans whose ancestors entered the U.S. through this venerable island passage.

> ELLIS ISLAND ATTRACTS 3 MILLION VISITORS EACH YEAR

A Midcontinent Gateway If the Statue of Liberty and Ellis Island are emblems of immigration to America from the Atlantic Ocean, St. Louis boasts a memorable monument that pays tribute to the nation's internal migrations: the Gateway Arch. In 1947 a group of St. Louis civic leaders, under the banner of the Jefferson National Expansion Memorial Association, launched a contest to design a monument commemorating the city's central role in the exploration of the American West following the 1803 Louisiana Purchase by President Thomas Jefferson, which added 828,000 square miles of land to the U.S. Eventually, that expanse of land would form all or parts of 15 states of the Union.

The contest was won by Finnish-American architect Eero Saarinen, whose vision was an exercise in simplicity that is now considered a landmark of Modernist design. Updating the notion of a triumphal arch from Roman and French antecedents for modern times, Saarinen envisioned a towering, inverted catenary arch (the shape assumed by a hanging metal chain supported at both

ends) that would run parallel to the Mississippi River. The Lewis and Clark Expedition, commissioned by Jefferson to explore the nation's new frontier, set out on its western journey in 1804 across the river from the arch. And viewed from the river, the arch frames the city's historic Old Courthouse, site of the 1847 and 1850 Dred Scott trials in Missouri that helped ignite the Civil War.

Fifty-one years old in 2016, the Gateway Arch, as it is commonly known, has become the indelible symbol of St. Louis, joining the ranks of such city-defining structures as the Eiffel Tower, the Great Pyramid of Giza and the Roman Colosseum. It is the tallest man-made monument in the U.S., 630 feet high, giving Jefferson bragging rights over Washington's monument. (The space between its legs at ground level, as mandated by the geometries of the catenary form, is also 630 feet.)

Yet if the arch succeeded in defining St. Louis as a modern city, it was often criticized: it was separated

conclusion of the first part of the master plan took place on Oct. 28, 2015—the 50th anniversary of the completion of the structure—celebrating the opening of the reshaped grounds around the arch, including a new park that crosses over the intrusive highway and finally connects the arch's grounds to the city's downtown.

In 2017 the Museum of Westward Expansion will complete its own westward expansion. It will receive a new name, the Gateway Arch Museum and Visitor Center; will boast a major new wing, which will add 40,000 square feet to the building's footprint; and will create a dramatic and welcoming aboveground entrance for it.

A Golden Door to the Pacific If the Gateway Arch is one of the world's great monuments, the Golden Gate Bridge in San Francisco is one of its most beautiful works of engineering, hailed as a masterpiece of design since it was dedicated in 1937. As its name suggests, the Golden Gate was the nation's western doorway, and those who passed through it included immigrants from China and other Asian nations, Forty-Niners caught up in the excitement of the Gold Rush, and young Americans bound for the Pacific Theater in World War II.

The famous bridge is not overseen by the NPS, but almost everything around it is, thanks to the establishment of the Golden Gate National Recreation Area in 1972. Unlike the majority of NPS properties, the Golden Gate grounds are not contiguous: rather, they are a collection of discrete holdings with great historical and environmental value, whose highlights include the famed island prison Alcatraz; the Presidio, a venerable fortress established by Spain in 1776 and run by the U.S. Army from 1846 until 1994; and the Muir Woods National Monument, north of San Francisco, the home of giant coastal redwood trees. Sprawling across some 80,000 acres of land and 59 miles of coastline, the recreation area is one of the largest urban parks in the world.

> **MORE THAN 14 MILLION PEOPLE VISIT GOLDEN GATE EACH YEAR**

Small wonder that this magnificent collection of holdings—did we mention the Golden Gate properties also include 1,200 historic structures, five National Historic Landmark districts, 13 National Register of Historic Places, five lighthouses and 365 archaeological sites?—attracts more than 14.5 million visitors each year.

There are other gateways in the U.S., from the nation's newest state, Hawaii, to its Canadian and Mexican borders. But the Statue of Liberty, Ellis Island, the Gateway Arch and the Golden Gate tell the story of America's growth unforgettably, from sea to shining sea.

from the city's civic center by a major highway, while its Museum of Westward Expansion was tucked underground, beneath the monument, and was much too small to convey the full story of St. Louis and the Western frontier in all its rich range and complexity.

As of 2016, that's changing: the parkland surrounding the arch is humming with machines and workers, as CityArchRiver, a public-private partnership that includes the NPS, is working to address these issues. The

Profile: Stephen T. Mather

The Critic Who First Led the Parks

How a wealthy executive helped preserve our wide-open spaces

AT THE END OF JOHN FORD'S CLASSIC 1962 film *The Man Who Shot Liberty Valance*, James Stewart, playing a U.S. senator who has lived through the pioneering days of the American West, is told by a newspaperman friend, "When the legend becomes fact, print the legend." And when it comes to Stephen T. Mather, the legend of how he became the first director of the National Park Service encapsulates the story of Mather's life so well that people have been printing it ever since.

As the story goes, Mather was a wealthy businessman who was also an enthusiast of the outdoor life and an advocate for preservation. California-born and a believer in conservation, he saw firsthand the extent to which the national parks of the West, then loosely administered, were being ravaged by business interests. Lumber companies felled entire first-growth forests, mineral companies strip-mined the land, and ranchers allowed domesticated sheep and cattle to fatten on the grasses of pristine meadows. In 1914, Mather, incensed, wrote a letter to Franklin K. Lane, the secretary of the Department of the Interior and an old friend, expressing his disappointment with the federal agency's management of the lands in the West set aside for preservation. Lane responded, "Dear Steve, If you don't like the way the parks are being run, come on down to Washington and run them yourself." And that's just what Mather did.

It's a fine yarn, whose only failing is its inaccuracy. The truth: Mather was a wealthy outdoor enthusiast who was indeed appalled by the state of California's parks. He and Lane were not classmates or friends—but

Mather did write to Lane about the condition of the parks, and Lane encouraged him to get involved in the effort to create a federal agency to oversee the properties then dubbed national parks but managed by states.

Mather, in fact, owed his prosperity to the immense natural resources of the West and his canny use of Western legend. Born in San Francisco in 1867, he was the son of Joseph W. Mather, a well-to-do businessman with deep roots on the East Coast, who was hired as the administrator of the Pacific Coast Borax Co., whose product was a mineral used in detergents and cleansers, mined from Death Valley in California.

Stephen Mather graduated from the University of California, Berkeley, and became a reporter for the *New York Sun* newspaper, then became advertising manager for his father's concern. The former journalist knew the value of a good human-interest story, and he persuaded the company to brand the Pacific Coast borax, essentially a commodity with no more value than anyone else's borax, as "20 Mule Team Borax," an allusion to the early practice of employing large teams of animals to haul copious amounts of the mineral out of the famed valley.

Print the legend? The Mathers branded the legend, and the Mathers, father and son, became wealthy—so wealthy that Stephen retired in his 40s and turned his attention to his longtime interest, the preservation of the scenery and resources of the West. Always a lover of nature, Mather had been drawn back to California over and over again in the first years of the 20th century. A disciple of John Muir's, Mather had joined the Sierra Club and become a prominent, active member in its advocacy for preservation.

So when the wealthy, gregarious and well-connected Mather contacted the Department of the Interior to encourage stronger conservation policies in the West, the agency was happy to enlist him in the battle.

Mather soon became the foremost advocate in Washington for the creation of a national parks agency, often using his own resources to hire staff, buy lands he then donated for preservation, and conduct public-relations efforts. Joined by another capable executive, Horace Albright, Mather twisted arms until he succeeded in his crusade on Aug. 25, 1916, when President Woodrow Wilson signed the legislation that established the National Park Service. Mather was named the first director of the NPS in May 1917, and in the years that followed, he led the agency with vision, flair and good judgment, winning wide respect for the fledgling organization—despite a long, debilitating battle with bipolar disorder.

Mather's leadership drew on all his experiences: his admiration for Muir and genuine love of the West; his mastery of advocacy, dating from his Sierra Club lobbying efforts; his journalistic knowledge that stories and fables can be powerful levers to move minds. Understanding that policymakers needed to experience the power of parks to fully appreciate their value, he led a successful effort to establish a series of national parks in states east of the Mississippi River.

Mather worked with railroads and automotive interests to provide increased access to the parks, and he and Albright established a nonpartisan, professional corps of executives and park rangers to administer the system of national parks and monuments, which nearly doubled in size on his watch. He resigned in 1929 and died in 1930. Albright succeeded him as director of the NPS, and he went on to support the placement of simple memorials to Mather in every national park, each bearing a phrase that is both legend and fact: "There will never come an end to the good he has done."

The 20-mule teams that hauled borax out of Death Valley became obsolete in 1889, only four years before Mather turned them into a romantic Old West legend.

Landmarks of
Discovery

Celebrating the visionaries
who took out patents on the future

SPEAKING TO MEMBERS OF THE U.S. SENate and the House of Representatives in his final State of the Union address on Jan. 12, 2016, President Barack Obama hailed America's heritage as a nation whose vision and industry had helped invent the future. "That spirit of discovery is in our DNA," the president declared. "America is Thomas Edison and the Wright brothers and George Washington Carver . . . America is every immigrant and entrepreneur from Boston to Austin to Silicon Valley, racing to shape a better world. That's who we are." Indeed it is. And the National Park Service, in its role as chronicler of the American experience, was already marching in step with the president. Each of the visionaries saluted in Obama's address is represented among the holdings of the NPS, including Thomas Edison National Historical Park in West Orange, N.J.; the Wright Brothers National Memorial in Kill Devil Hills, N.C.; and George Washington Carver National Monument in Diamond, Mo.

These institutions are devoted to illuminating the life and times of creative geniuses who helped shape history.

Wright Brothers National Memorial, North Carolina *Above, Orville Wright takes to the air in 1911 on the Outer Banks. At left, life-size statues at Kill Devil Hills capture the jubilation of the first flight in 1903.*

But the NPS's commitment to celebrating every aspect of American culture extends far beyond the realm of science and invention. National monuments, historical sites and landmarks commemorate the achievements of those who left a mark on American culture in a wide variety of fields, including the pioneers of jazz in New Orleans and such beloved American writers as Edgar Allan Poe, John Steinbeck and Ernest Hemingway. The holdings of the NPS honor social activists ranging from the founders of the women's suffrage movement and the leaders of the civil rights movement of the 1950s and '60s and celebrate such iconic figures of U.S. life as Pony Express riders, Gold Rush prospectors, the Tuskegee Airmen and the women factory workers of World War II.

Birthplace of Aviation Visitors to the Wright Brothers National Memorial on North Carolina's Outer Banks can experience in the most direct way possible the Ohio brothers' quest to fly. The memorial invites us to walk in their footsteps; feel the sharp, wing-lifting winds that blow inland from the Atlantic Ocean; and trace their first flight from beginning to end—not a very challenging journey, given that Orville Wright, who was at the controls of the brothers' *Flyer* on Dec. 17, 1903, when it lifted off for the first time, flew the craft for a total of 120 feet, remaining in the air for 12 seconds.

Sculptor Stephen H. Smith memorably captured the moment when humans first took to the skies: working from the Wright brothers' own photographs of their process, he re-created the last seconds before the *Flyer* took wing with life-size statues of the brothers, their assistants and a few onlookers, just as the scene was captured by the camera. The result is a stirring evocation of ordinary men caught up in an extraordinary adventure—and to see youngsters step into the past and interact with the statues in the place where history was made is to see the process of inspiration in action.

The Haunts of a Modern Wizard No inventor changed the trajectory of history more than the gifted,

Thomas Edison National Historical Park, New Jersey *The Edison lab in New Jersey includes machine shops where models were tooled, above. At near left is the first movie studio, "Black Maria," mounted on tracks to revolve and capture sunlight. At far left, Edison poses in 1910, age 63.*

intensely driven, highly competitive—and famously ornery—Thomas A. Edison. The sheer list of Edison's inventions is exhausting: from his first major innovation, an improved ticker-tape machine he sold to the Gold & Stock Telegraph Co. in 1871, he moved on to create the incandescent lightbulb, the phonograph, the movie camera, and the process of electrical power generation and transmission.

Perhaps the most influential of Edison's innovations was his revolutionary approach to the process of invention itself. He was the pioneer of what we now call research labs, facilities in which Edison and his experts in a variety of fields—from electricity to sound recording to

moving pictures to manufacturing techniques—collaborated to create technologies that made once-unreachable dreams into modern products: recording the human voice for playback, capturing slow-motion images of a man sneezing, illuminating living rooms with electrical power.

Breakthrough inventions of this sort flowed from Edison's laboratory in West Orange, N.J., over the course of decades. And today visitors to Thomas Edison National Historical Park can trace Edison's progress as he and his assistants pursued their dreams. The NPS site includes the laboratories in which Edison and his corps of inventive geniuses toiled, as well as his nearby 29-room Victorian mansion, Glenmont, filled with personal memorabilia and a host of cutting-edge technologies that one would expect from a man who seemed to live with one foot in the future.

The park headquarters are located in the Laboratory Visitor Center, which received a major renovation in 2009, making Edison's lab much more accessible. Visitors were once herded through the facility in packs; now they are invited to wander through it on self-guided audio tours that trace the entire arc of Edison's career.

> THE EDISON HOLDINGS INCLUDE SOME 5 MILLION DOCUMENTS

The holdings include early kinescopes, the one-person viewing machines that showed short moving pictures, as well as a restored version of the world's first movie studio, where the films were shot. Nicknamed "Black Maria," owing to its resemblance to a police wagon, this ramshackle structure was covered in tar paper to allow filmmakers to control the source of light within. A large section of its roof could be propped open to allow sunlight to flood the space when desired, and the building was mounted on a track that allowed it to revolve so as to follow the sun's path across the sky.

Edison was so prolific for so long—he lived from 1847 to 1931—that the records of his life's work constitute a vast archive of correspondence, product designs, business papers and news clippings. By far the largest single collection of Edison materials, the site includes 300,000 physical items and more than 5 million documents.

"Black Leonardo" If the NPS's Edison holdings are immense, its tribute to the third of Obama's trio of visionaries, the celebrated "Peanut Wizard," George Washington Carver, is a triumph of simplicity. The pocket-size memorial, located well off the beaten path outside the small town of Diamond in southwestern Missouri, welcomes visitors with a simple bust of Carver. There is no headquarters building: the main attraction is a one-mile hike that leads visitors across grasslands, wooded groves and a small stream on the farm where the young Carver, an African American born into slavery during the Civil War, first discovered his love of nature, a moment captured in a fine statue on the hiking trail.

TIME described Carver as a "black Leonardo" in 1941. Rising from poverty, he earned a master's degree in agriculture from Iowa State University, where he hoped to teach, before being wooed away by the well-known black university the Tuskegee Institute in Alabama. Carver taught there for 47 years, supervising experimental farms and managing a laboratory that discovered hun-

George Washington Carver National Monument, Missouri *Above, a cast-bronze statue of Carver as a boy, by the late Robert Amendola, is the focus of the small but inspiring memorial near Carver's early home.*

dreds of new uses for a wide variety of plants, in particular the peanut and sweet potato.

The Carver memorial is a far cry from the wide-open spaces of a Yellowstone, Yosemite or Denali. But it's a good reminder that the NPS is the custodian not only of immense spaces and irreplaceable national monuments like the Statue of Liberty and the Jefferson Memorial but also of hundreds of unprepossessing historic sites that celebrate America's history simply and quietly, minus Barnum, braggadocio and ballyhoo.

Like any other tourist, off-duty ranger Banks snaps a selfie as he hikes through Olympic National Park in Washington State.

In the Footsteps of John Muir

Exploring the joys and challenges of life as an NPS ranger

THE CALL OF THE WILD: THAT'S THE summons, often heard at an early age, that draws many Americans to serve as National Park Service rangers. It's a good bet that if you were to attend the Ranger Rendezvous, the big annual get-together of the Association of National Park Rangers, you'd hear a lot about those tempting calls from the attendees. There's the intense love for the outdoors, often cultivated from youth through family camping trips and hikes. There's an appreciation for nature's processes and the natural sciences: botany and zoology, geology and meteorology. There's the urge to share one's passion, to watch young minds marvel at how a caterpillar becomes a butterfly; how an owl's head swivels so he see behind him; or how wind, glaciers and rivers can carve rock into a host of

eerie forms: pinnacles and canyons, arches and mesas. And often there's admiration for such heroes of the conservation movement as John Muir and Rachel Carson.

Tom Banks, 56, who has been a ranger for more than 30 years, serves as the treasurer of the ANPR, and he fits the profile. "I grew up in Massachusetts," he told TIME in 2016. "When I was a youngster, my parents, my brothers and sisters and I went on camping trips in the Western national parks, and the photographs from those trips made a lasting impression on me. Early in my teenage years, I wanted to return to these places and experience them more deeply."

And so Banks went West, and his first brush with the NPS was working as a parking-lot attendant at Rocky Mountain N.P. "I did a lot of camping growing up and began backpacking in New Hampshire's White Mountains. Being outdoors was what interested me most, and by the time I was 15 I knew I wanted to be a ranger. When I went on guided walks in national parks, I tagged along right behind the rangers and told them I was aiming to be one of them. They always took the time to talk to me, and they encouraged me."

Banks's journey through the park system has taken him through seasonal work in many of the most spectacular parks in the nation: Glacier, Denali, Redwood, Sequoia and more. But he has spent the most time at Olympic N.P. in Washington, which includes regions of an unusual ecological system, the rare temperate rain forest, located above the equator, where mist is king and the days get warm but not sweltering.

Ask Banks to pick a favorite park, and he acts like a father requested to name his favorite child: that's not going to happen. "It's impossible to pick a favorite. They each have important stories to tell and inspiration to give." As for education and outreach to the public, Banks takes particular pride in the series of entertaining videos he helped create to educate visitors on park etiquette. "I have spent five years volunteering for the Appalachian Trail Conservancy, having a role in producing educational media teaching 'Leave No Trace' principles and techniques to leave the outdoors as good as we find it. That work has been enormously gratifying. I want to encourage people to be 'conscious' users of the outdoors." To take a look at the result, visit *goo.gl/wzFLsC*.

Banks deeply admires the life and teachings of John Muir, and he has assumed Muir's character in appearances to promote ecological principles. Asked how he prepares to take on the role, he says, "Impersonating John Muir has been one of the really fun projects of my lifetime. To get in the mood to portray him, I spend several days re-reading his writings, and I go for walks in nature, dressed in old-fashioned garb, and I imagine how he'd respond to what I'm seeing and hearing and feeling."

Banks also shares Muir's interest in natural sciences. Botany is of particular interest to him, and he earned a master's degree on the subject of subalpine lakes, which grounded him in the geology of the parks. Asked about the future of the parks, he replies, "Threats to parks vary according to their location. Many parks are threatened by air pollution drifting in from neighboring regions and from across the Pacific Ocean. Climate change is taking its toll on wildlife, plant life and glaciers. Visitors feeding wildlife leads to unnatural, unhealthy wildlife behavior that ends up harming the animals. So there's something we can all do to help parks—from large-scale, like carpooling to work, riding a bike and walking more—to small acts, like keeping our food secure from wildlife when we're in a park."

For Banks, "having wide-open places that are unchanging except for the forces of nature, and having historic places that are touchstones to our cultural past—these, to me, are the greatest benefits that national parks provide. These are places of emotional and spiritual solace, of remembering the way things have been—and the values we learn from the outdoors we want to maintain. As for hiking and climbing, I like the advice I heard a long time ago: 'Only push yourself to 80% of your physical limits when you're outdoors. Keep something in reserve, so if something unexpected happens, you've got enough energy to work through the challenge. Tread carefully out there.'"

Wise words from a veteran ranger. But Banks himself may not practice what he preaches: as communicator, teacher and Muir impersonator, he gives himself 100% to the job he loves. His message to young readers: if you find yourself feeling the call of the wild, visit *anpr.org* and join the ranks of America's dedicated rangers.

In his 33 years as a ranger, Banks has spent the most time in Olympic N.P., part of which is a rare biosphere for North America: a temperate, not tropical, rain forest.

Of Monuments and Memorials

The obligation to remember America's honored dead gets a powerful contemporary update

IN ITS ROLE AS ONE OF THE PRIMARY KEEPERS of the American people's national memory, the National Park Service addresses one of its most delicate functions: to honor those who perished in conflict or at the hands of terrorists and to create shrines where people can assemble to bear witness, to learn, to pray. In the past decades, beginning with the building of the Vietnam Veterans Memorial in Washington, which opened in 1982, our memorial spaces have undergone a powerful metamorphosis. Out went the classical architectural memes long associated with

death, honor and remembering—the classical pillars and statues, the carved oak and acanthus leaves, the rusting armaments, which would have been at home in the Athens of Pericles. In came powerful new architectural forms based on modern, abstract styles, as well as a focus on the sacrifices of specific individuals rather than a generic abstraction, all enlivened by new technologies that bring the act of memory to life in fascinating new ways.

In 2000, TIME writer Roger Rosenblatt, seeing for the first time the Oklahoma City National Memorial that recalls the slaying of 168 Americans, observed, "Memorials

have always been useful to societies to establish and confirm common values, to send messages to posterity about what is significant and worth preserving. Statues, tombs, arches, pyramids, obelisks: all have stood for abstractions such as heroism, sacrifice and valor. A place like the Oklahoma City National Memorial or the Vietnam Veterans Memorial can send its own messages by challenging the simplicity of such values. By questioning what has been appreciated without examination—the glorification of war, for instance—a monument becomes a statement of values itself. Old memorials used to honor permanence.

Newer ones treat permanence as an illusion."

Had Rosenblatt been writing after the digital revolution changed the way we communicate and learn, he might have added that new technologies have allowed the NPS, in its role as custodian of history, to reach out to people in ways that might have seemed magical only decades ago. Museums and memorials are no longer treated as distinguished attics where Grandpa's old uniform can safely be stashed. Now they are living, thrilling spaces, animated by technologies that create powerful new ways to understand and honor the past.

Vietnam Veterans Memorial, Washington *Reflections in the wall help visitors become part of the story.*

The NPS operates some 263 monuments and memorials to the battles that shaped the nation. They range across history: a farmhouse from the Battle of Saratoga (N.Y.) in the Revolutionary War; Valley Forge, Penn., where Washington's starving soldiers camped in the winter of 1777–'78; the site of the 1794 Battle of Fallen Timbers in today's Ohio, which drove Native Americans from the era's northwestern frontier; the great Civil War battlefields whose names still move us: Antietam and Gettysburg, Chattanooga and Chickamauga.

The memorials include places and events that acknowledge the darker sides of the nation's history. They include the sites of massacres of Native Americans by white settlers; the battles of the Civil Rights movement of the 1960s; the rude camps where Japanese Americans were incarcerated during World War II, a policy long judged to be a stain on the nation's honor. The memorials are wonderfully diverse and inclusive: the Rosie the Riveter World War II Home Front National Historical Park in Richmond, Calif., offers a tribute to the millions of women who worked in factories during that conflict. The Manhattan Project National Historical Park honors three facilities where workers toiled to

> SOME MEMORIAL SITES ADDRESS DARK TIMES IN U.S. HISTORY

create the atom bombs that ended World War II. Some monuments even conserve artifacts from battles never fought: the Minuteman Missile National Historic Site in South Dakota preserves a Cold War–era complex whose intercontinental ballistic missiles were never launched.

Wall of Honor No conflict in U.S. history proved more problematic to honor than the Vietnam War, the lengthy conflict in Southeast Asia that ended with the withdrawal of U.S. troops from South Vietnam in 1975 and the takeover of that nation by its communist rival, North Vietnam. The stinging defeat ended a war that had bitterly divided the nation, and for years the notion of honoring the sacrifice in a conflict in which some 2.7 million Americans served, and some 58,000 died or were casualties, seemed unlikely.

The monument that was eventually built, though originally denounced by many, is now one of the most moving memorials in the U.S., and it has provided the template for an entirely new approach to such sites. In November 1982, seven years after the end of the war and amid a great deal of controversy, a V-shaped memorial wall composed of black granite and sunk into the ground on the National Mall near the Lincoln Memorial, was formally dedicated.

The structure was the brainchild of Yale University undergraduate Maya Lin, only 21 when she won a national competition to design the monument, which was criticized by many for its abstract, austere, forward-looking design, which avoided the classical styles long used in memorials. But once dedicated, the wall quickly became a living shrine. Visitors traced the names of their friends or kin with their fingers, or rubbed pencils over them to capture the name on paper. Here was a memorial that touched people, because people touched it. And thanks to Lin's artistry, while staring at the names of their loved ones in the massive polished

> **THE NUMBER OF NAMES ENGRAVED ON THE VIETNAM WALL: 58,307**

wall, people could see their own image in the reflective stone, making themselves part of the memorial.

The wall further came to life as a memorial once the public began decorating it with personal memorabilia.

Visitors soon began leaving items—photos and notes, military medals—beneath the names of fallen loved ones, at the base of the wall. Each day, those offerings are removed with care. Nonperishable items are stored in an NPS archive—and as of 2016, more than 400,000 such offerings were held in storage.

In 2015 the NPS and partner the Vietnam Veterans Memorial Fund (VVMF), the congressionally mandated group that spearheaded the building of the memorial, announced a program that will allow viewers to take a vir-

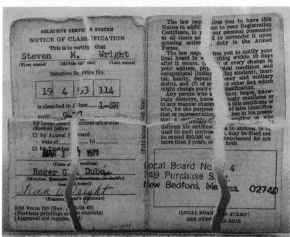

The thousands of artifacts collected by NPS personnel at the Wall include, clockwise from top left: bracelets with the names of U.S. soldiers listed as missing in action, and a Purple Heart medal. Dog tags are among the artifacts most frequently left at the wall. A draft card lists a young American's status as deferred until graduation from high school.

tual journey through these highly personal items, making the sacrifices of the war available to a much wider audience than ever before. The site, *vvmf.org/items*, features some 500 memorial offerings.

"This is a collection of the people, by the people, and now available for the people to honor the service of all Vietnam veterans and remember the sacrifice of those who gave all," said Jim Knotts, president and chief executive officer of VVMF, when the site went live. The online gallery is another example of how the NPS and its partners are using new technologies to tell the American story in memorable ways. The website also serves as a preview of the contents of a proposed Education Center at the Wall, which will contain as many as 6,000 such items. Fund-raising efforts are well under way for the center; those seeking more information can visit the website at *buildthecenter.org*.

> **THE WWII MEMORIAL OPENED 59 YEARS AFTER THE WAR'S END**

A Belated Salute Surprisingly, it took Americans almost six decades to honor the veterans of a war that united, rather than divided, the nation: World War II. That conflict ended with the triumph of the U.S. and its allies on two fronts, in Europe and the Pacific. But perhaps because the war was fought almost entirely on foreign soil and at sea, no national monuments to victory were created in the U.S., aside from the U.S.S. *Arizona*–Valor in the Pacific National Monument in Hawaii, site of the Japanese surprise attack on the U.S. naval base at Pearl Harbor, which sent the U.S. to war.

By the late 1980s, many veterans of the war were in their 60s and 70s, and Americans gradually realized that their sacrifice in the war must be commemorated while its veterans were still alive. The legislative effort to build a national World War II memorial began in Congress in 1987, under President Ronald Reagan, and was signed

National World War II Memorial, Washington
Critics disliked the clutter of the World War II memorial, as well as its location on the National Mall, which is managed by the National Park Service.

into law in 1993 by President Bill Clinton. The process of designing, approving and building the memorial required 11 years, almost three times the length of the war itself. But on May 29, 2004, the National World War II Memorial was dedicated by President George W. Bush.

Recognizing the significance of the war to U.S. history, the new memorial was located on a key position on the National Mall in Washington, halfway between the Lincoln Memorial and the Washington Monument. Some say the monument, designed by Friedrich St. Florian of Rhode Island, suffers from mission creep: it includes 56 granite pillars, representing the 48 U.S. states at the time of the war, as well as seven U.S. territories, including future states Alaska and Hawaii—and the District of Columbia. Two arched pavilions reflect the war's two theaters of combat, the Atlantic and the Pacific, while a fountain offers relief from this martial array

HONOR FLIGHTS HAVE BROUGHT THOUSANDS OF VETS TO SEE THEIR TRIBUTE

of stone. This was your grandfather's version of a memorial; then again, it was your grandfather's generation that was being honored.

Architecture critics were not kind. TIME's Richard Lacayo dismissed the memorial as "purest banality." The *Philadelphia Inquirer* described it as "pompous" and compared it with the edifices of Hitler and Mussolini, the enemies in the war. The *Washington Post* piled on, calling it "overbearing and bombastic."

If the World War II memorial were to come alive as a moving, living tribute to veterans, it seemed that such emotions would have to be brought to it. And that's just what happened, thanks to the Honor Flight program, created by a physician from Springfield, Ohio, Earl Morse. His patients included several World War II veterans who hoped to visit the new memorial but found the expense and physical burdens too costly; the

Oklahoma City National Memorial *The memorial chairs of bronze, stone and glass are illuminated at night.*

veterans who had been in their 60s when the memorial was first proposed were now in their 80s.

Morse was an aviation enthusiast and amateur pilot, and he enlisted volunteers from his local aviation club to fly area veterans to Washington. In May 2005, six small planes flew 12 veterans to the capital for a visit to the new monument. The response of both the veterans and the volunteers who flew and accompanied them was so powerful that the Honor Flight program began to attract national attention.

With a boost from Jeff Miller, a North Carolina businessman whose father and uncle were World War II veterans, the program soon became a nationwide organization, flying leased airplanes and harnessing a network that includes thousands of volunteers and NPS personnel, to give aging veterans a chance to see the memorial they so memorably earned. Honor Flights often conclude with a "Heroes' Welcome" arrival ceremony at local airports, as veterans returning from the nation's capital receive a rousing welcome as they are cheered by their fellow citizens.

Victims of Terrorism In recent decades, Americans have had to address the challenge of creating memorials

> THE OKLAHOMA CITY MEMORIAL INCLUDES A FIELD OF 168 CHAIRS

not only for soldiers and sailors who died in battle but also for victims of a more modern plague, terrorism. The bombing of a federal office building in the heart of Oklahoma City by homegrown terrorists led by U.S. Army veteran Timothy McVeigh in 1995 was the first terrorist act to demand commemoration. The bomb devastated the Alfred P. Murrah government office building, damaged 300 other structures, killed 168 people, including 19 children attending the facility's day-care center, and wounded more than 650 other victims.

The Oklahoma City National Memorial, designed by the Butzer Design Partnership, then based in Berlin, was dedicated on April 19, 2000, five years after the tragedy. It incorporates many of the lessons learned from the Vietnam Veterans Memorial. The outdoor site honors each of the victims of the blast individually, in the form of a sculptural bronze, stone and glass chair that are are illuminated at night, lending a numinous glow to the scene of past horror.

The field of chairs is framed by two massive bronze gates at either end of a reflecting pool: the 9:01 Gate and the 9:03 Gate, their lettering resembling a digital clock. The minutes signify the times just before and after the

Flight 93 National Memorial, Pennsylvania *High walls deliberately screen the crash site from approaching visitors.*

explosion. The hour of 9:02 is represented by the chairs. The overall effect is powerfully somber and respectful; TIME hailed the new memorial as one of the Ten Best Designs of 2000 after it was opened to the public.

Jetliner Revolt Only six years after the Oklahoma bombing, Americans were shaken by the terrorist attacks of Sept. 11, 2001, when Al Qaeda agents hijacked four passenger jets and used two of them as guided missiles to attack the Twin Towers of Manhattan's World Trade Center and a third to damage the Pentagon in Washington. A fourth plane, United Airlines Flight 93, was intended to wreak further havoc, but the passengers on the plane, alerted to their plight by cellphones, rose up against the hijackers.

THE FLIGHT 93 VISITOR CENTER OPENED ON SEPT. 10, 2015

"Let's roll," one of the passengers cried, as a group of volunteers used a beverage cart to batter down the cabin door, attack the hijackers and bring the craft down outside the small town of Shanksville in eastern Pennsylvania, killing 40 passengers and four terrorists. The passengers' bravery saved untold lives that might have been lost had the craft plowed into its target in Washington.

It took 14 long years, but on Sept. 11, 2015, the Flight 93 National Memorial was dedicated as the newest me-

morial operated by the NPS. Designed by Paul Murdoch Architects of Los Angeles, it employs abstract architecture, individual biographies and the latest technologies to tell the story of the passengers' heroism.

A black granite path leads visitors up a gentle rise to two 40-foot-tall concrete walls that evoke the shape of airplane wings even as they obstruct the view that lies beyond them. As visitors pass through narrow openings in the walls, they see for the first time a sweeping view of the field where the jetliner hit the ground at more than 560 mph: it is a brilliant use of architecture as revelation.

Within the visitor center, recordings of the phone calls from the hijacked craft, as well as life-size replicas of the seats in the cabin and a series of animated videos, tell the story of the passengers' revolt on Flight 93 in memorable and illuminating detail. The use of modern technologies is eye-catching, yet something that can't be seen at the memorial is even more important: the public-private partnership that was forged among the National Park Service, the Families of Flight 93 group, the federal Flight 93 Task Force and many other partners, both local and national, that worked together to ensure that the sacrifice of 40 brave souls would never be forgotten.

Soskin, 94, told TIME: "Our visitors are hungry for history and for stories of the old days."

Sharing History, Beyond the Fables

The oldest park ranger may be the feistiest as well

TUESDAY, NOV. 17, 2015, BEGAN LIKE ANY other day for National Park Service ranger Betty Reid Soskin. In the morning, she was preparing to deliver a presentation to 55 high school students who were visiting the Rosie the Riveter/WWII Home Front National Historical Park in Richmond, Calif. The lights darkened as Soskin started to run a brief orientation film about the park. That's when she was interrupted and asked to report to the office of Tom Leatherman, superintendent of the park.

Once there, she was handed a phone, and ... well, let's let Betty tell the story in her own words. "At the other end of the line was director Jon Jarvis of the National Park Service, calling from Washington to announce an invitation for me to attend the tree-lighting ceremony at the White House with the First Family on December

3rd! Not only that, but I was being asked to introduce the president of the United States of America! I was stunned." But introduce the Obamas she did, with a much-worn picture of her great-grandmother, who was born into slavery, in her pocket. As Betty said later, "My bucket list has disappeared, pretty much."

Reader, perhaps you've guessed by now that Betty Soskin isn't an ordinary ranger. At 94 in 2016, she is the oldest full-time living park ranger in America—and likely the liveliest. Already a well-known figure in Richmond ("Betty is the iconic face" of the park, Richmond mayor Tom Butt declared), Soskin came to national attention in 2013, when a congressional deadlock partially shut down the federal government and closed the doors of the Rosie the Riveter NHP. On her blog, which she updates almost daily, Soskin told the legislators to come to their senses and end the gridlock: at her age, she said, she was running out of time and didn't want to waste any more of it sitting at home. Her involuntary furlough was picked up by the national media, and before too long, Soskin became a celebrity.

Soskin's great-grandmother was born in 1846, and Betty, born in 1921, got to know her well. When Soskin was 20, she was swept up in the war effort, like every other American. But though Richmond, a factory town, turned out ships and weapons for the military, Betty was not a Rosie the Riveter. "That really is a white woman's story," Soskin said, noting an aspect of the war that's often forgotten: many of the factories were racially segregated. So Soskin took a job as a clerk for the all-black auxiliary of a segregated boilermakers union.

After the war, Soskin and her husband bought a house in an all-white neighborhood and received death threats for doing so. She was politically active and a noted song-writer during the civil rights movement in the 1960s, and later was a community organizer. When Soskin first heard of the proposed historical park in Richmond, she volunteered to serve on the planning committee. After all, as she observed, "what gets remembered is a func-tion of who's in the room doing the remembering."

Speaking to TIME in 2016, Betty told the rest of the story. "When I first got involved in the planning stages to develop the park, the emphasis was strictly going to be on the 'Rosie the Riveter' gals who worked in the big assembly plants," she said. "I explained to the others on the devel-opment committee that I had been refused the opportunity to work as a 'Rosie' because I was African Ameri-can. Instead, I worked as a clerk within a racially segregated group. I explained that I thought the park and museum could explain a much larger swath of history than just the Rosie stories. I urged them to tackle many more subjects raised by the American experience in the war.

"I said the museum should teach younger generations about the past, straight from the mouths of people like me, who actually lived through the past and can shed some light upon it—those of us who have come so far and have had so much to come through.

"I told them we should tell the story of Japanese Americans who were sent off to internment camps during the war, because that's part of the American story as well. And they agreed. Every week, we show a film about those events. I always attend the film and speak to the audience about my memories of those days.

"I told my fellow committee members about how Henry Kaiser, the big industrialist, brought thousands of African Americans from the five Deep South states to work in the Bay Area. He brought 98,000 Southern-ers to Richmond, a town of 23,000 before the war. There were 130,000 people in this city at the war's end, and about 30% of them were African Americans. The fact that these black and white Southerners would not be sharing drinking fountains, housing, schools, any public accommodations back in their places of origin for another 20 years—that wouldn't happen until the 1960s—shows how the war accelerated the pace of social change. We had tens of thousands of people in Richmond who started out as sharecroppers and ended up building the ships that helped end the war."

Leatherman, Soskin's friend and boss, told TIME that Betty was the most gifted interpreter of history he had ever worked with. "She tells a much broader story about America, and the experience of African Americans, and she's telling about things she lived through. It's so compelling and convincing; our visitors are riveted by her." But don't tell Betty what Leatherman said. She'll just remind you that she's never been a riveter.

Soskin at the museum. "Whatever cynicism I've felt as an African American tends to evaporate" when she speaks to youngsters, she wrote on her blog.

Credits

COVER PHOTOGRAPHS
Front cover, Grand Teton National Park: Matt Anderson/Moment/Getty Images. Back cover, Grand Canyon National Park: 2/Robert Glusic/Ocean/Corbis

TITLE PAGE
1 Dennis Flaherty/Getty Images

CONTENTS
3 (Top to bottom, left to right) iStockphoto/Getty Images; Blaine Harrington III/Corbis; David Epperson/Getty Images; iStockphoto/Getty Images; Richard Ellis via ZUMA Wire/Corbis; Francesco Riccardo Iacomino/Moment/Getty Images; Steve Simonsen/Getty Images

INTRODUCTION
5 George Ranalli/Photo Researchers/Getty Images

GUARDIAN OF THE NATION'S SPIRIT
6 Sean Crane/Minden Pictures/Corbis 8 Alan Copson/JAI/Corbis 10 Michael Nichols/National Geographic Creative/Getty Images 12 Stuart Westmorland/Corbis 14 Michele Falzone/JAI/Corbis 16 Douglas Peebles/Corbis

AMERICA'S CROWN JEWELS
18 Golden Gate, Yellowstone National Park by Thomas Moran, 1893, oil on canvas, Buffalo Bill Historical Center, Cody, Wyoming/Photo by Corbis 20 Old Faithful by William Henry Jackson; albumen print, 1870/Photo by GraphicaArtis/Getty Images 21 (Left to right) Fotosearch/Getty Images; Oscar White/Corbis; Corbis; Library of Congress Prints & Photographs Division 22 National Park Service 23 (Top to bottom, left to right) Work Projects Administration Poster Collection/Library of Congress (2); Courtesy of Doug Leen (2); Work Projects Administration Poster Collection/Library of Congress; Courtesy of Doug Leen (3) 24 Bettmann Corbis 25 Linda Davidson/The Washington Post via Getty Images

THE NPS, BY THE NUMBERS
26 Graphic by Laura Stanton/LaVidaCo Communications; Photo illustration (background image) Jeff R. Clow/Getty Images; Insets (from left) Cchoc/iStockphoto/Getty Images; John & Lisa Merrill/Getty Images; Kevin Moloney/Getty Images; A.L. Christensen/Getty Images; Erik Petersen/For The Washington Post via Getty Images 27 (Top, from left) Universal Images Group/Getty Images; Frans Lanting/Mint Images/Getty Images (Bottom, from left) Doug Merriam/MCT via Getty Images; Ron Watts/Getty Images; Eyezaya/iStockphoto/Getty Images; Katkami/Moment Open/Getty Images; Mmphotos/Getty Images

PRESERVING AMERICA'S SINGULAR SPACES
28 Modoc Stories/Aurora Photos 30 Kennan Harvey/Aurora Photos 31 Richard T. Nowitz/Corbis 32 Luciana Whitaker/LatinContent/Getty Images 33 (From top) Tony Gervis/Aurora Photos; David Clifford/Aurora Photos 34 Phil Schermeister/National Geographic Creative/Getty Images 35 Harrison Shull/Aurora Photos 36 (From top) Michael Hanson/Aurora Photos; Nicolaus Czarnecki/ZUMA Press/Corbis 37 Skip Brown/National Geographic Creative/Getty Images 38 Corey Rich/Aurora Photos 39 Corey Rich/Aurora Photos 40 Sumio Harada/Minden Pictures 41 Stephen Frink/Corbis

42 Radius Images/Corbis 43 (Clockwise from top) David H. Carriere/Getty Images; Jim Brandenburg/Minden Pictures/Corbis; Tim Fitzharris/Minden Pictures 44 Patrick J. Endres/AlaskaPhotoGraphics/Corbis 46 Sunny Awazuhara-Reed/Design Pics/Corbis 47 (From top) Joe Raedle/Getty Images; Sandra Leidholdt/Moment Open/Getty Images; Lucky-Photographer/iStock/Getty Images 48 Library of Congress/Science Faction/Getty Images 49 PhotoQuest/Getty Images 50 Julia Kuskin/Cultura/Getty Images 51 Stuart Palley/ZUMA Press/Corbis 52 (From top) David S. Boyer and Arlan R. Wiker/National Geographic/Getty Images; Westend61 GmbH/Alamy 53 Adam Burton/Getty Images 54 Don Pitcher/Getty Images 55 Dave and Les Jacobs/Blend Images/Corbis 56 Library of Congress Prints & Photographs Division 57 Underwood & Underwood/Corbis 58 Debra Behr/Alamy 60 G. Brad Lewis/Getty Images 61 Jose Fuste Raga/Corbis 63 Menno Boermans/Aurora/Getty Images 64 © Ansel Adams Publishing Rights Trust/Corbis 65 Roger Ressmeyer/Corbis 66 © Ansel Adams Publishing Rights Trust/Corbis 67 © Ansel Adams Publishing Rights Trust/Corbis

PRESERVING AMERICA'S HERITAGE
68 Karen Bleier/AFP/Getty Images 70 Tetra Images/Getty Images 72 (From top) Terry Mathews/Alamy; René Mattes/Hemis/Corbis 73 Thinkstock/Getty Images 74 Dennis Hallinan/Alamy 76 Michael Lawenko Dela Paz/Flickr RF/Getty Images 78 Corbis 79 Ralph Crane/The LIFE Picture Collection/Getty Images 80 Russell Kord/Alamy 81 Popperfoto/Getty Images 82 (Clockwise from top) Walter Bibikow/JAI/Corbis; Danita Delimont/Alamy; Mondadori Portfolio via Getty Images 83 © RGB Ventures/SuperStock/Alamy 84 Courtesy of Tom Banks 85 Michael Melford/National Geographic/Getty Images 86 Dan Thornberg/iStockphoto/Getty Images 88 Drew Angerer/The New York Times/Redux 89 Michael S. Williamson/The Washington Post via Getty Images (4) 90 Jon Hicks/Corbis 92 Sarut Panjavan/Getty Images 93 Michael S. Williamson/The Washington Post via Getty Images 94 Justin Sullivan/Getty Images 95 Justin Sullivan/Getty Images

TIME

Editor Nancy Gibbs
Creative Director D.W. Pine
Director of Photography Kira Pollack

America's National Parks
Editor Kelly Knauer
Designer Ellen Fanning
Photo Editor Patricia Cadley
Copy Editor Bruce Christopher Carr
Research Tresa McBee
Production Rich Shaffer

Time Inc. Books

Publisher Margot Schupf
Associate Publisher Allison Devlin
Vice President, Finance Terri Lombardi
Vice President, Marketing Jeremy Biloon
Executive Director, Marketing Services Carol Pittard
Director, Brand Marketing Jean Kennedy
Finance Director Kevin Harrington
Assistant General Counsel Andrew Goldberg
Assistant Director, Production Susan Chodakiewicz
Senior Manager, Category Marketing Bryan Christian
Brand Manager Katherine Barnet
Associate Prepress Manager Alex Voznesenskiy
Project Manager Hillary Leary

Editorial Director Kostya Kennedy
Creative Director Gary Stewart
Director of Photography Christina Lieberman
Editorial Operations Director Jamie Roth Major
Senior Editor Alyssa Smith
Assistant Art Director Anne-Michelle Gallero
Copy Chief Rina Bander
Assistant Managing Editor Gina Scauzillo
Assistant Editor Courtney Mifsud

Special Thanks Brad Beatson, Nicole Fisher, Erin Hines, Kristina Jutzi, Seniqua Koger, Kate Roncinske